Traditional And Modern Art Tattoos

Guide To Drawing Traditional And Modern Tattoo Art

Art Tattoo

By : Gala Publication

Published By :

Gala Publication
© Copyright 2015 – Gala Publication

ISBN-13: **978-1522707295**
ISBN-10: **1522707298**

Table of Contents

FAIRY TATTOO

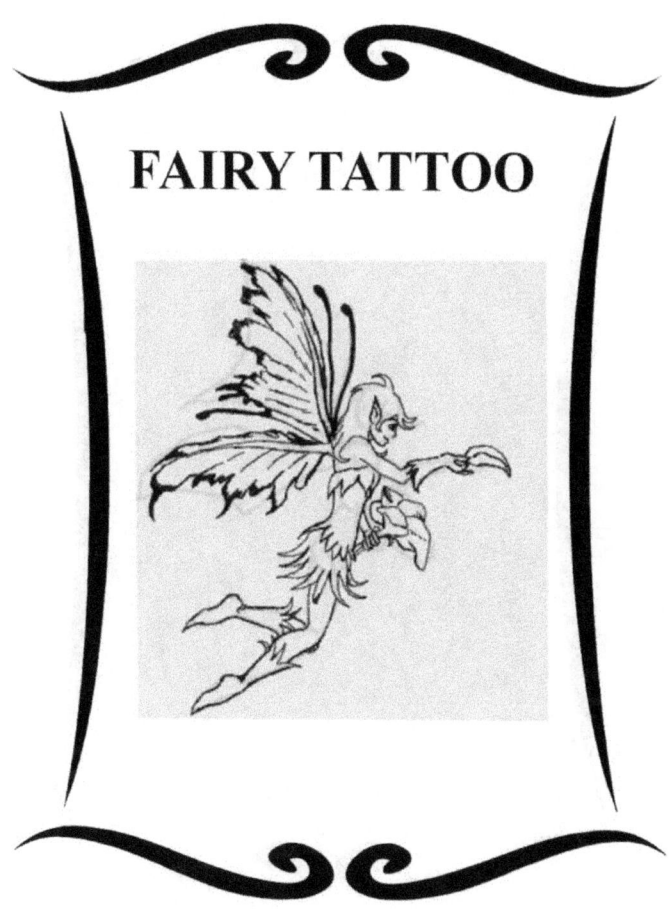

6

STEP 1

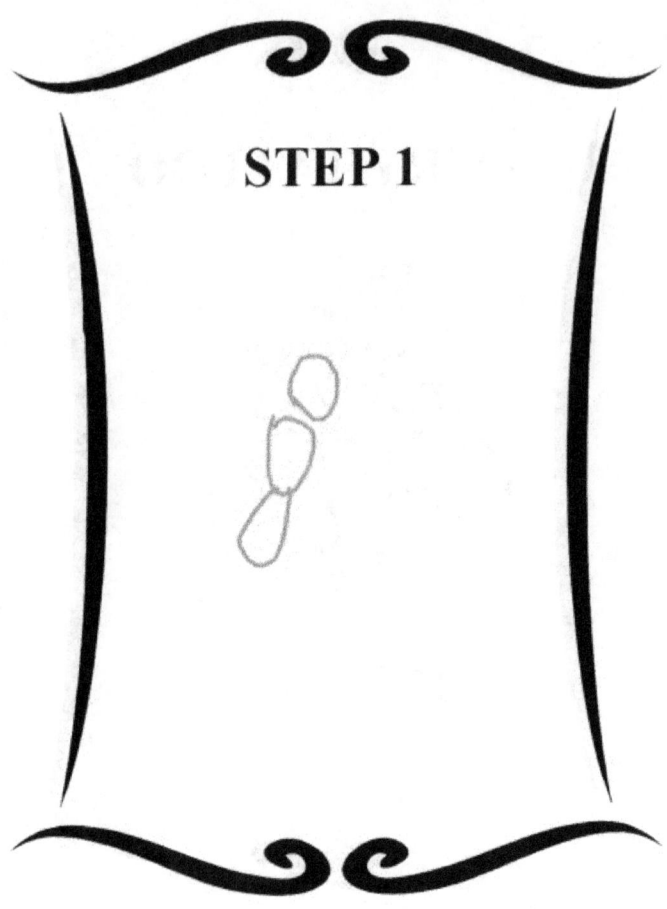

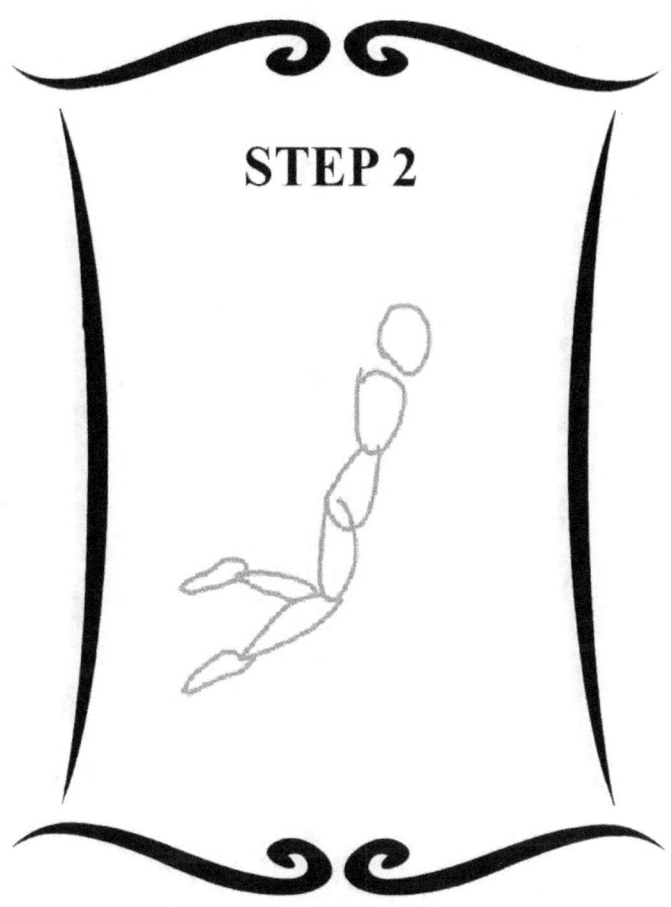

STEP 2

STEP 3

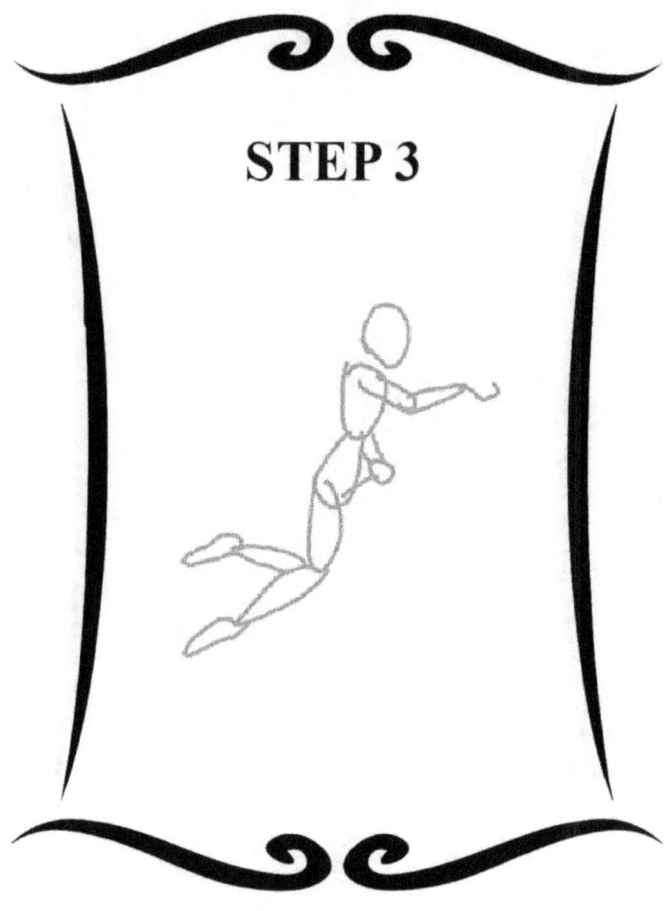

STEP 4

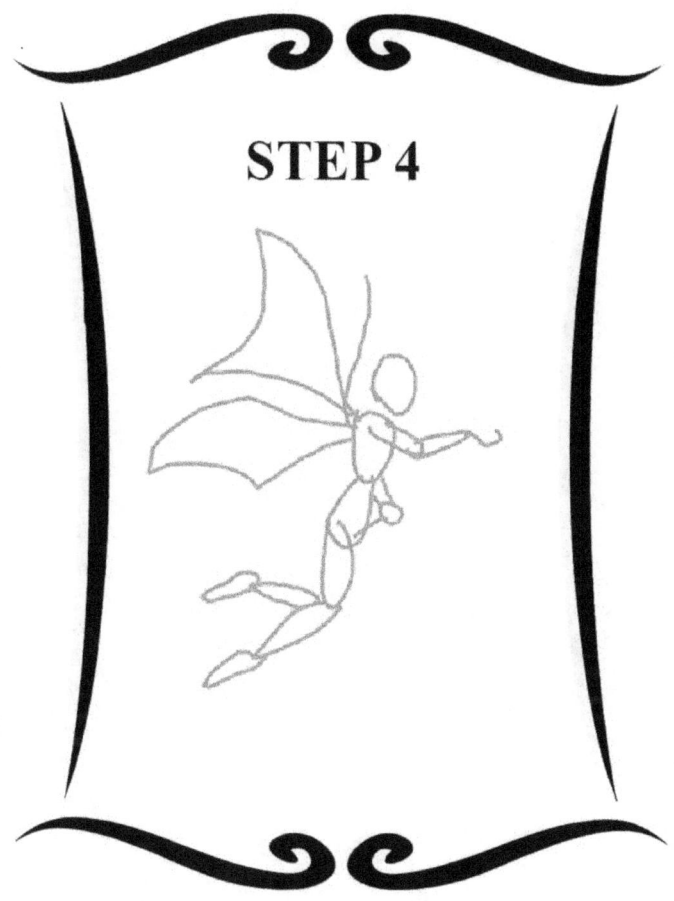

STEP 5

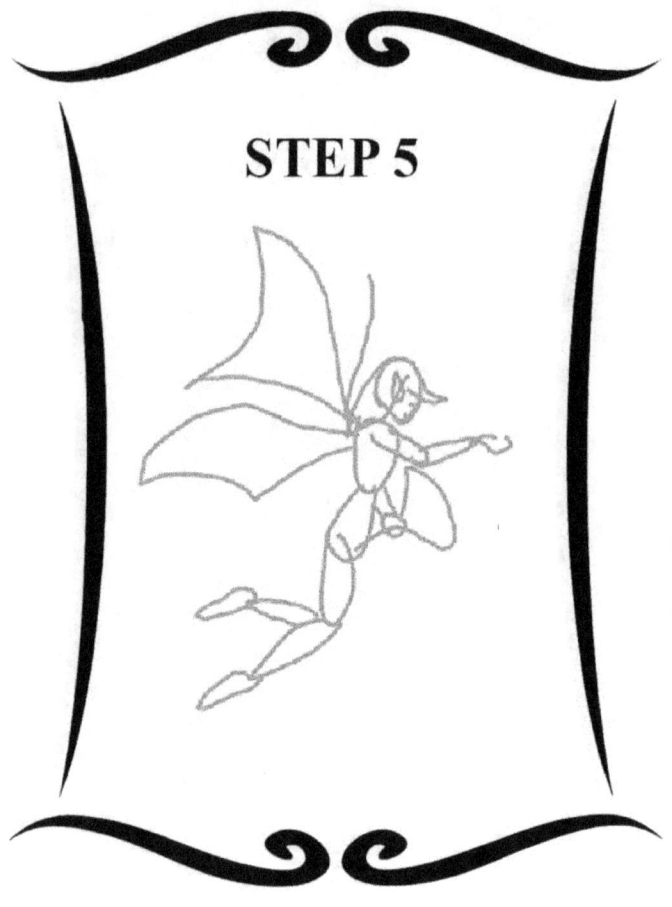

STEP 6

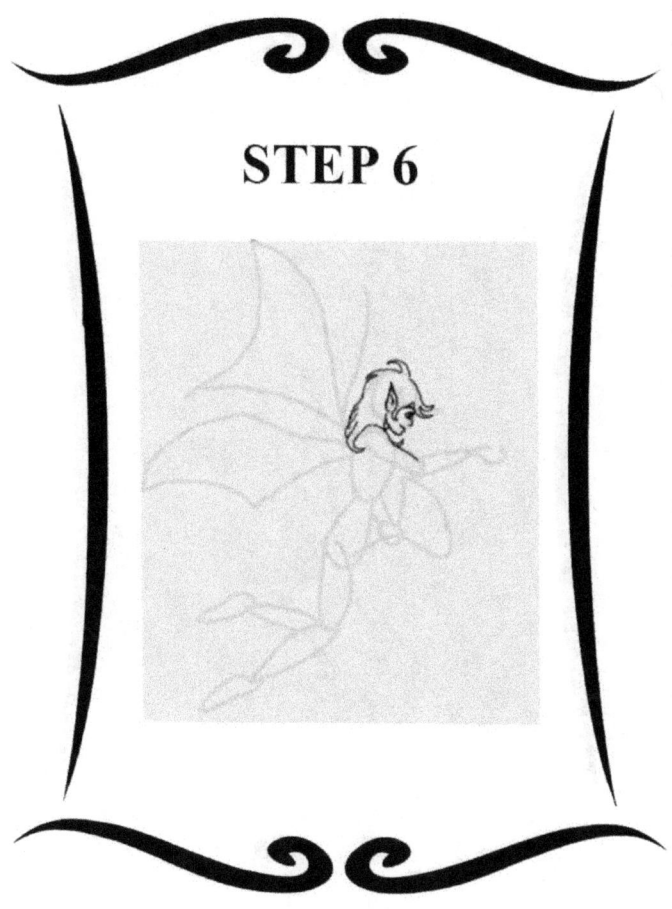

STEP 7

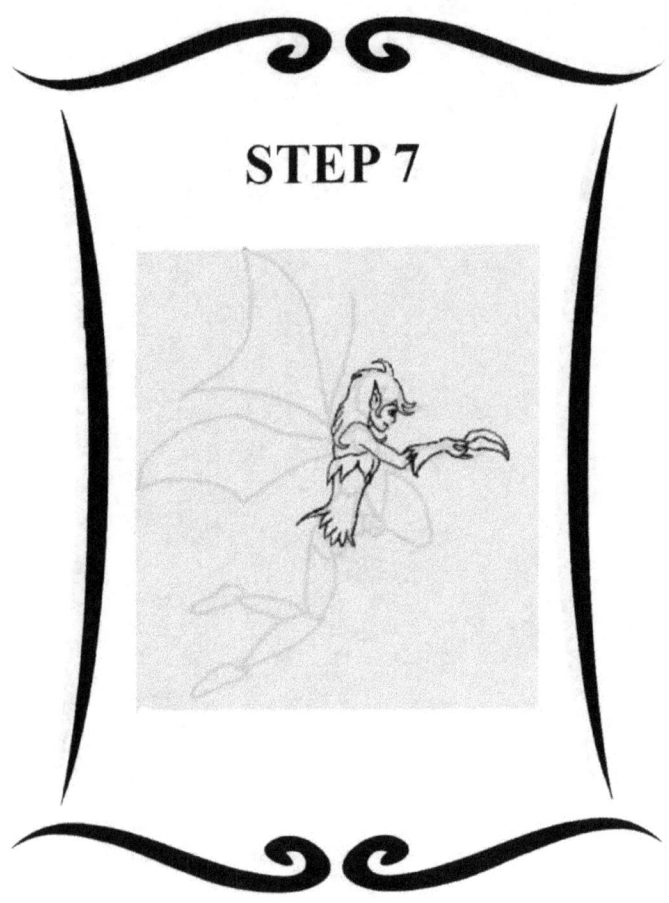

STEP 8

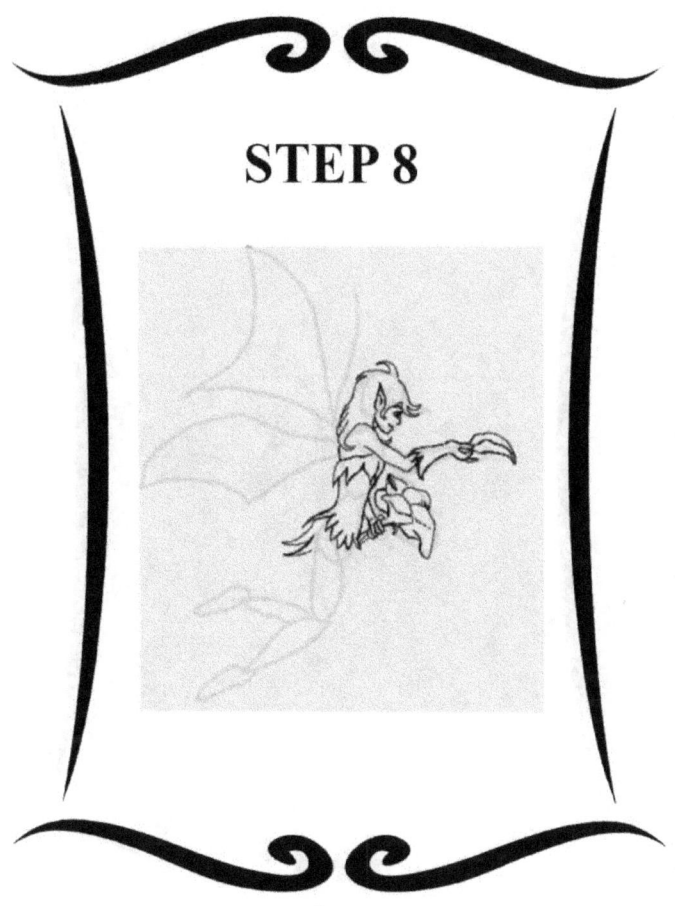

STEP 9

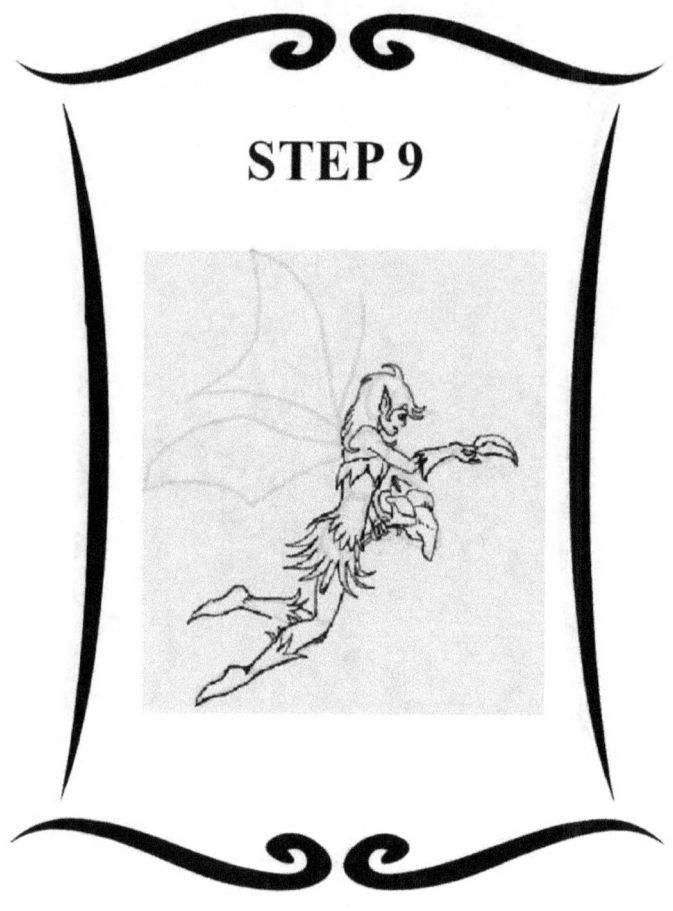

STEP 10

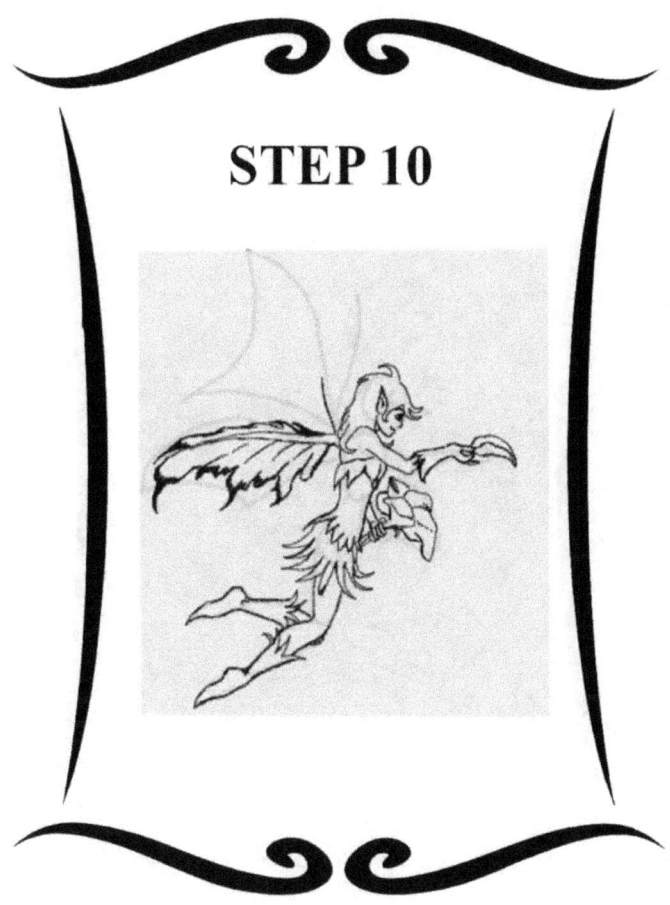

STEP 11

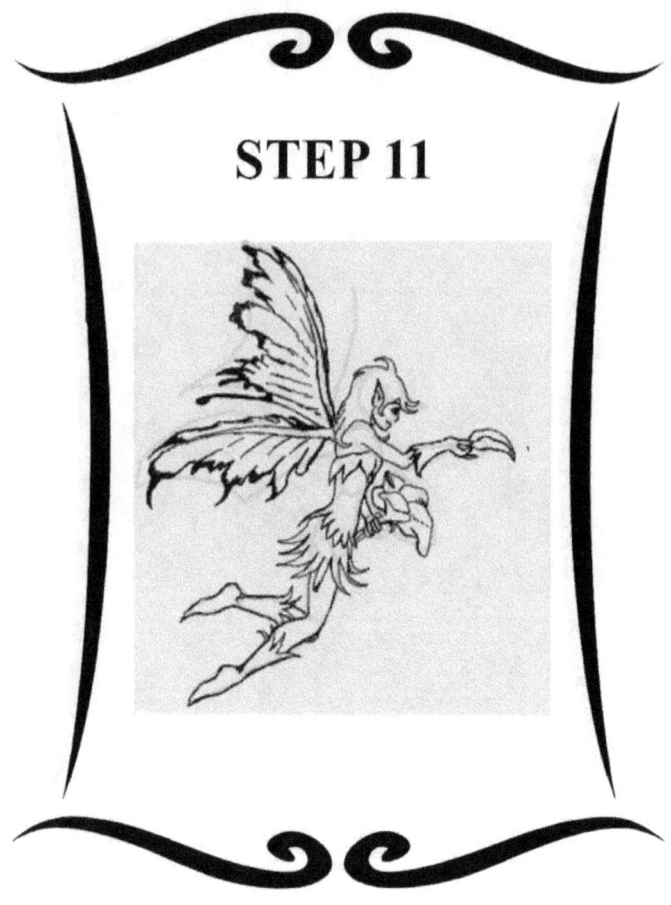

STEP 12

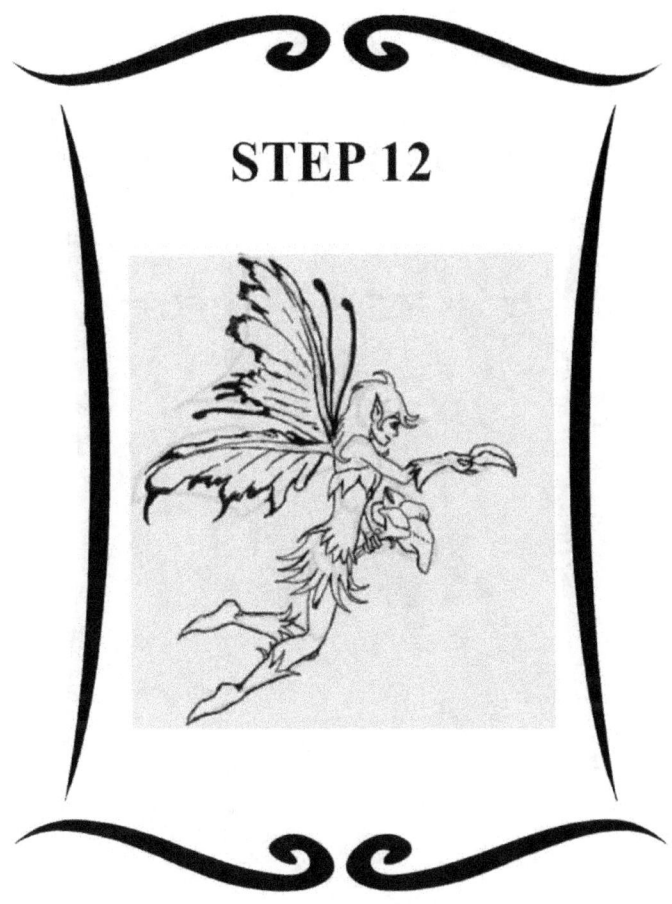

FEATHER TATTOO

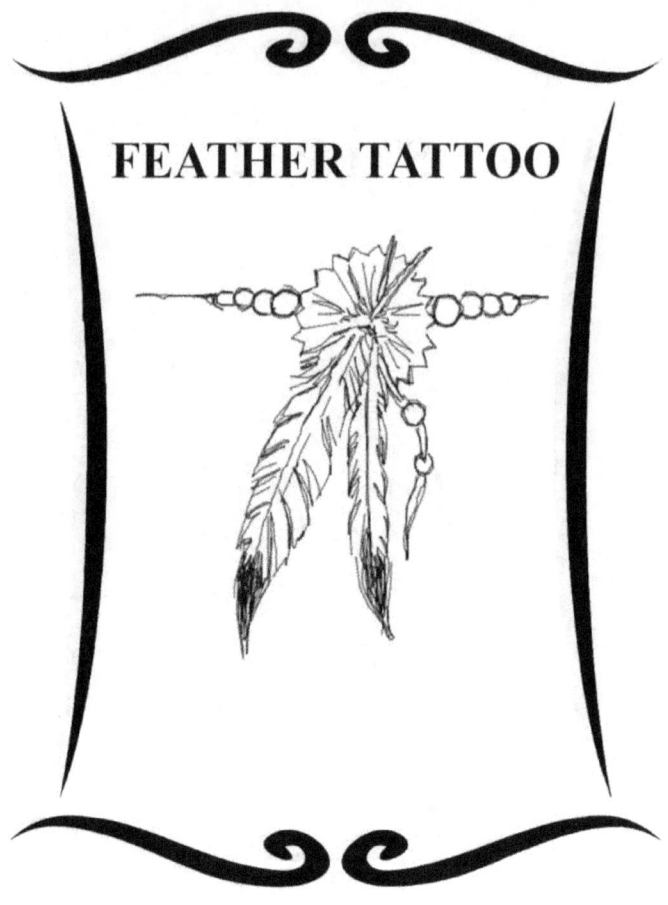

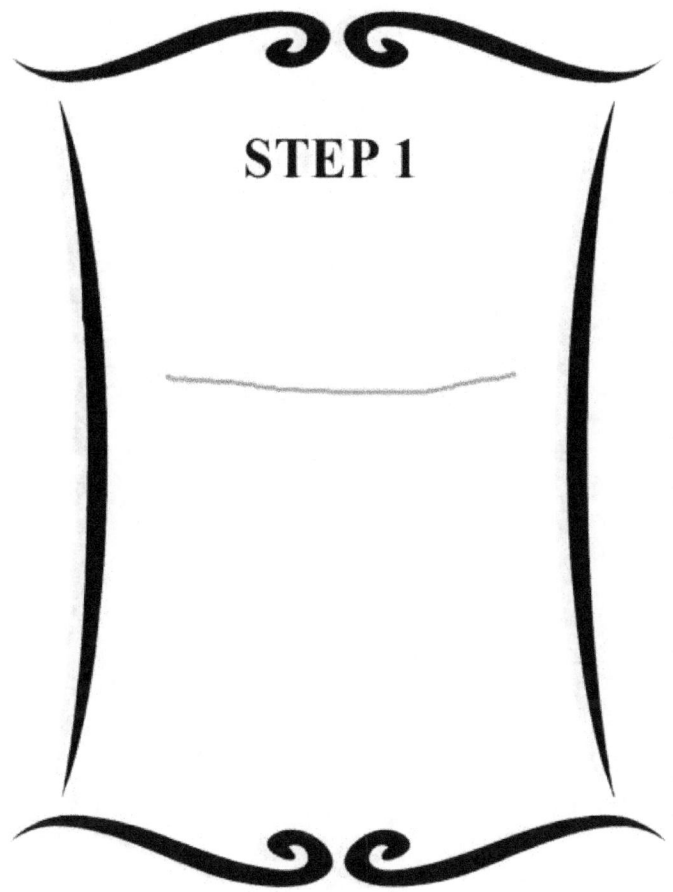

STEP 1

STEP 2

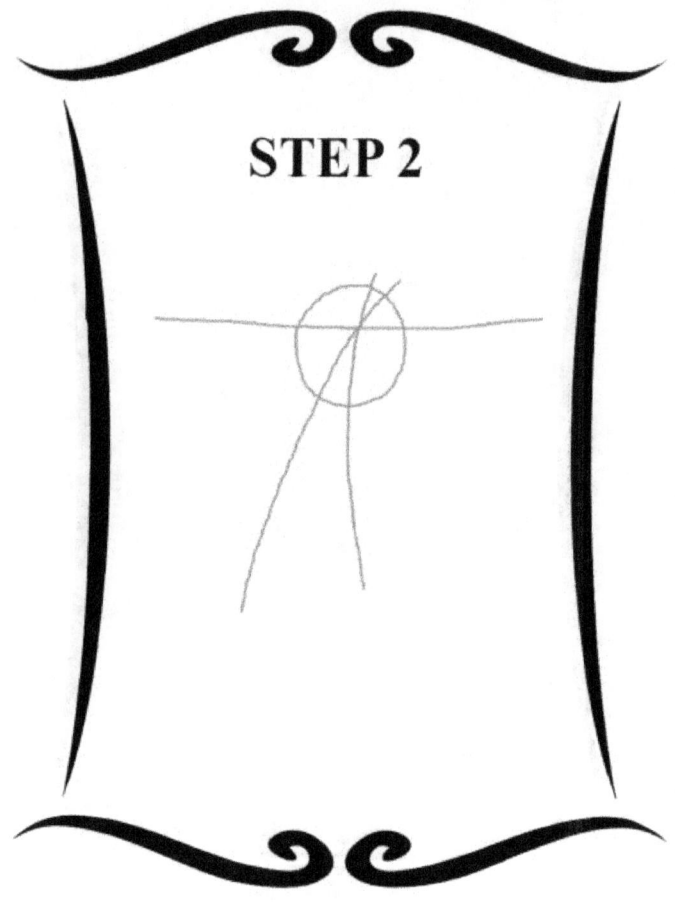

STEP 3

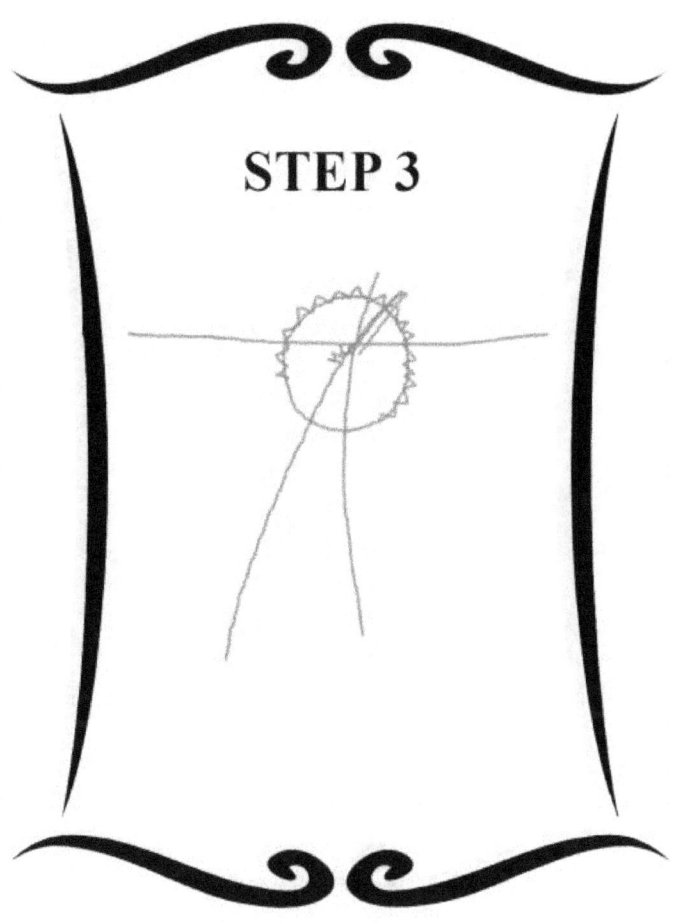

STEP 4

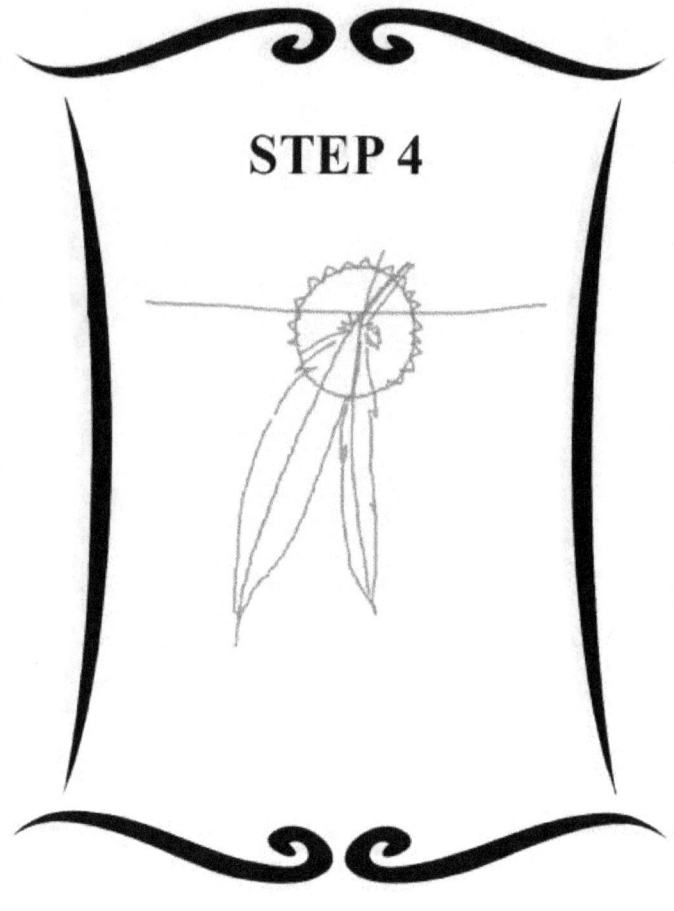

STEP 5

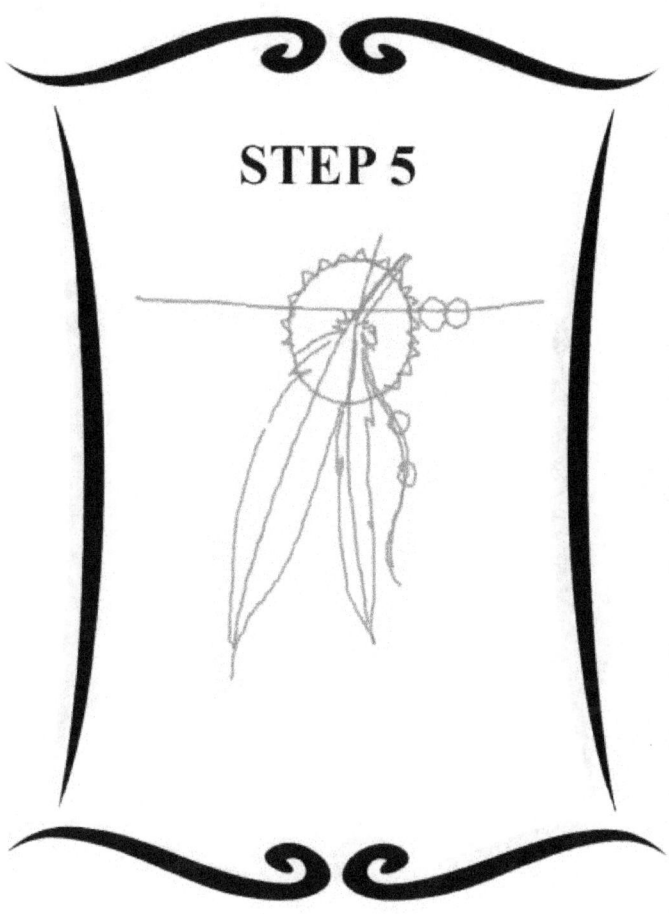

STEP 6

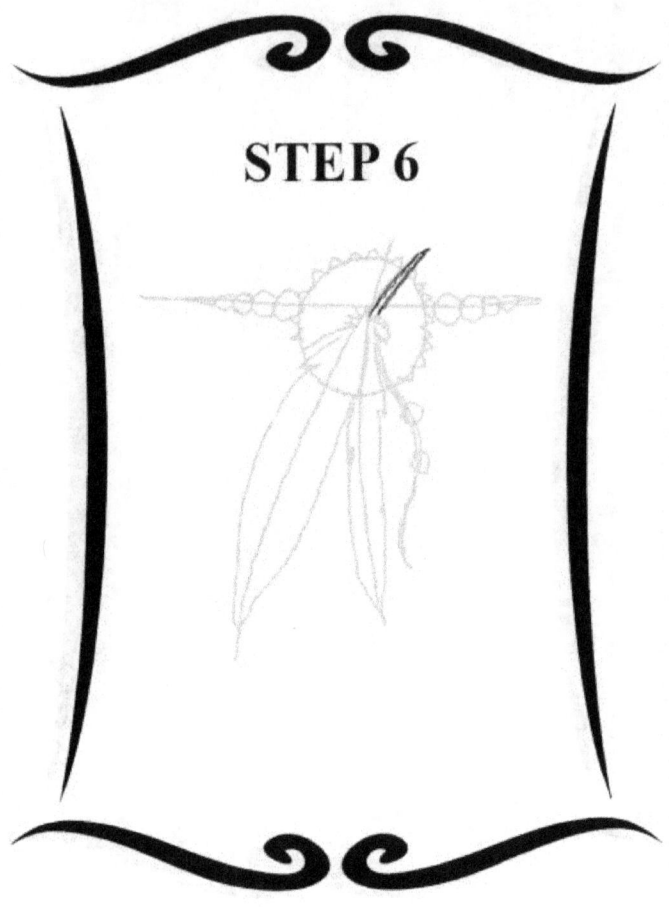

STEP 7

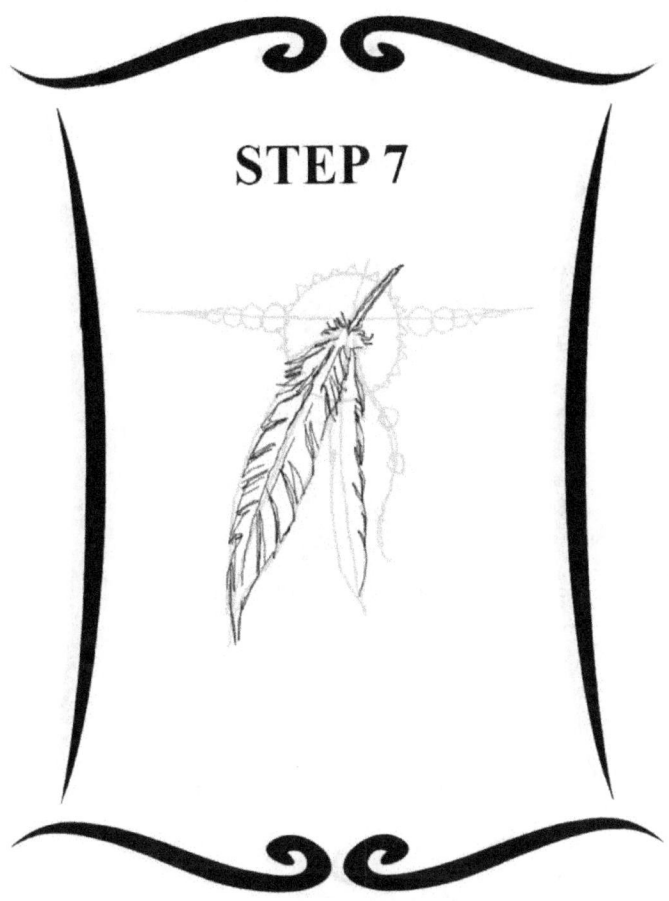

STEP 8

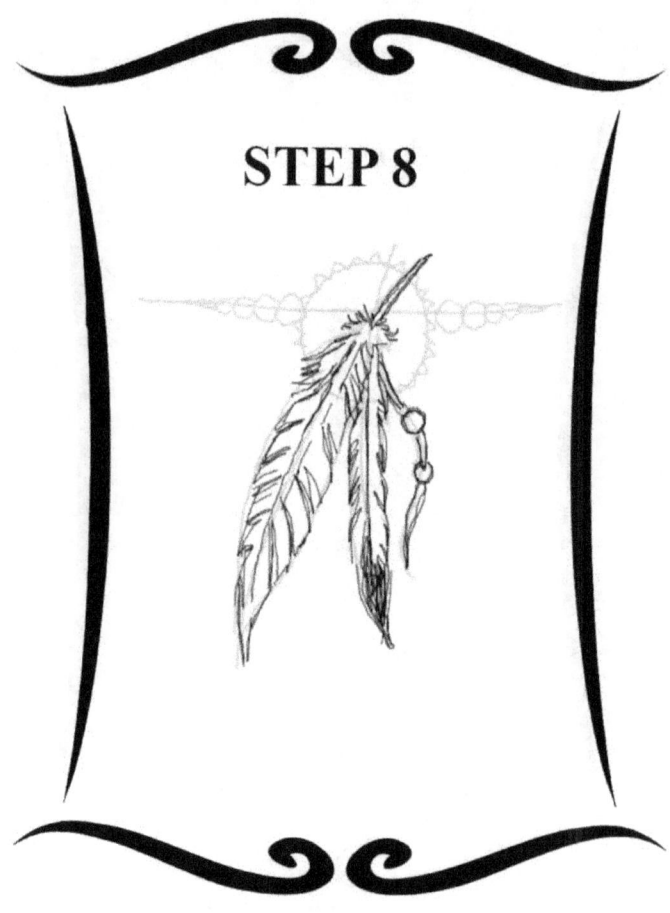

STEP 9

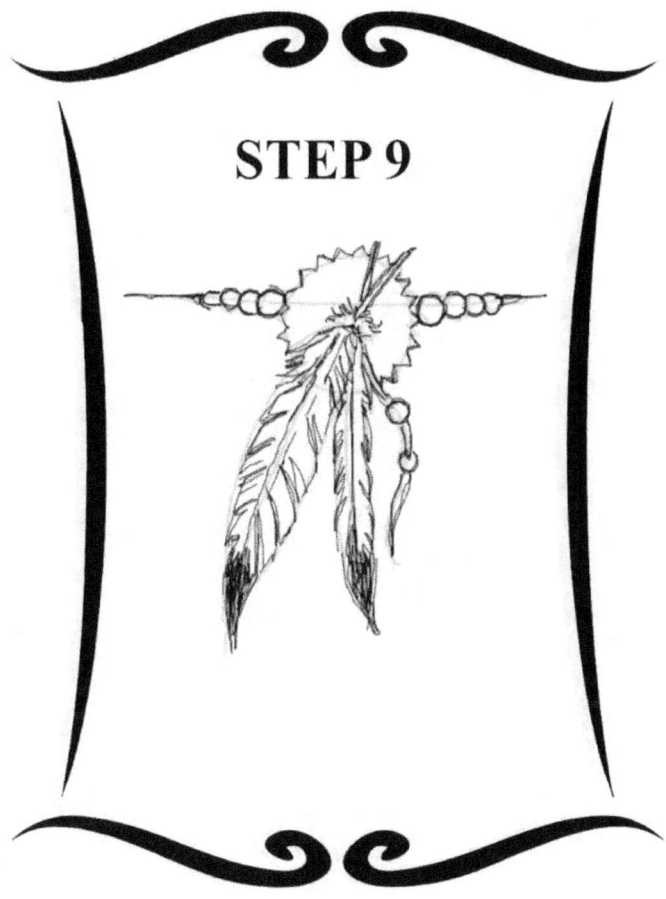

STEP 10

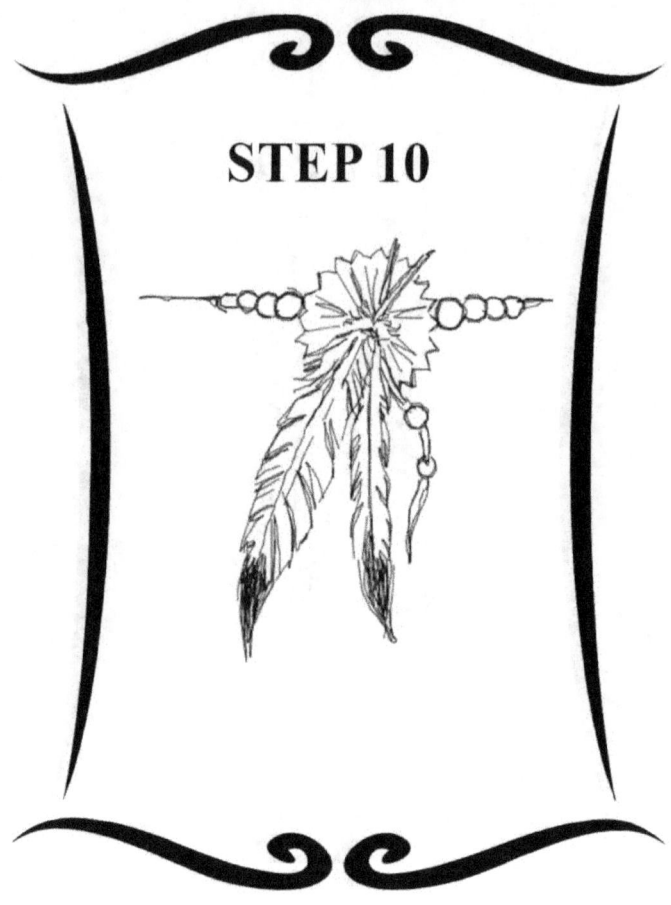

LOVE TATTOO

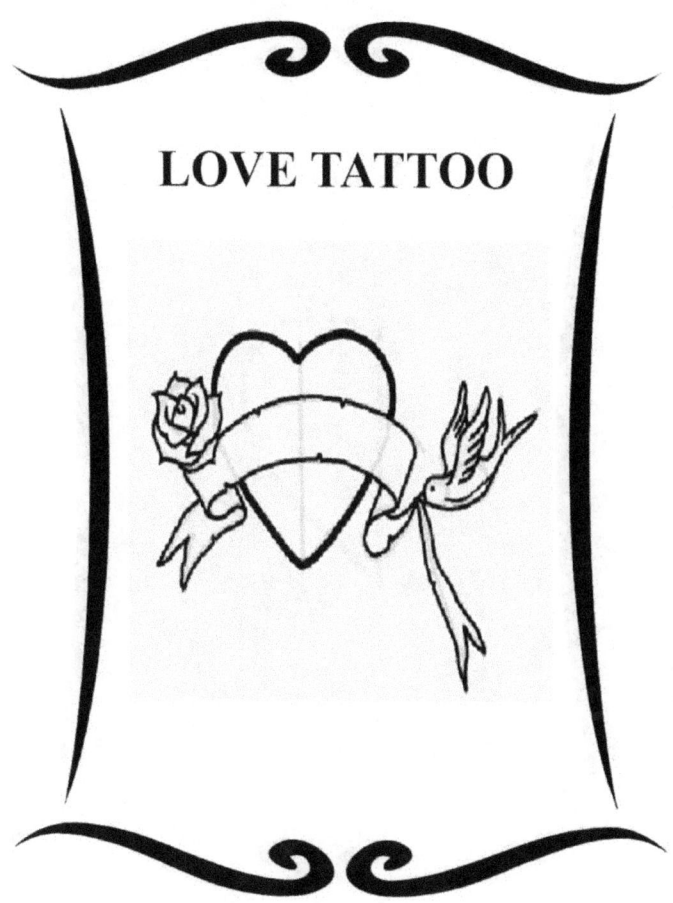

STEP 1

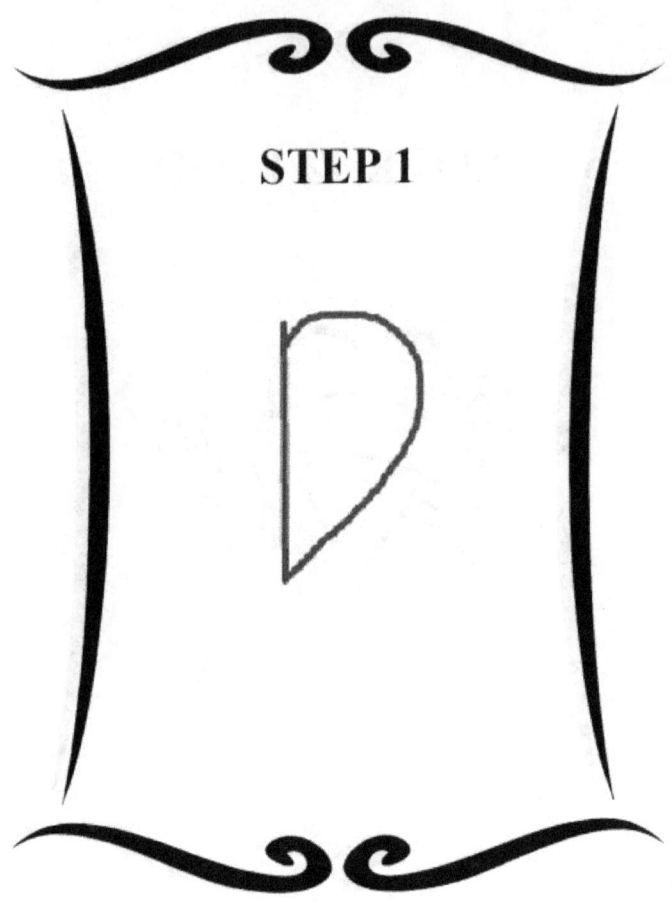

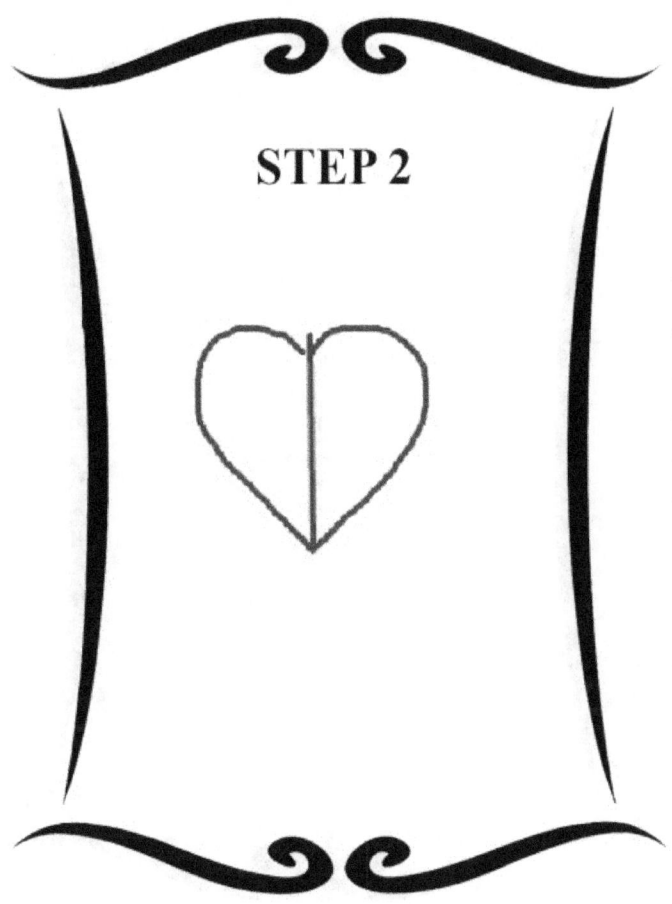

STEP 2

STEP 3

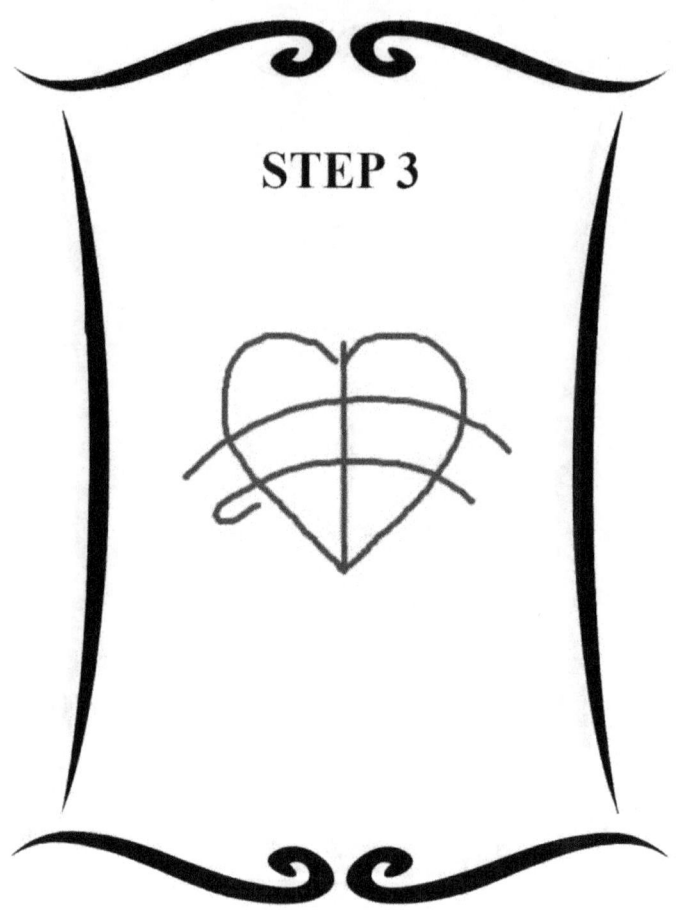

STEP 4

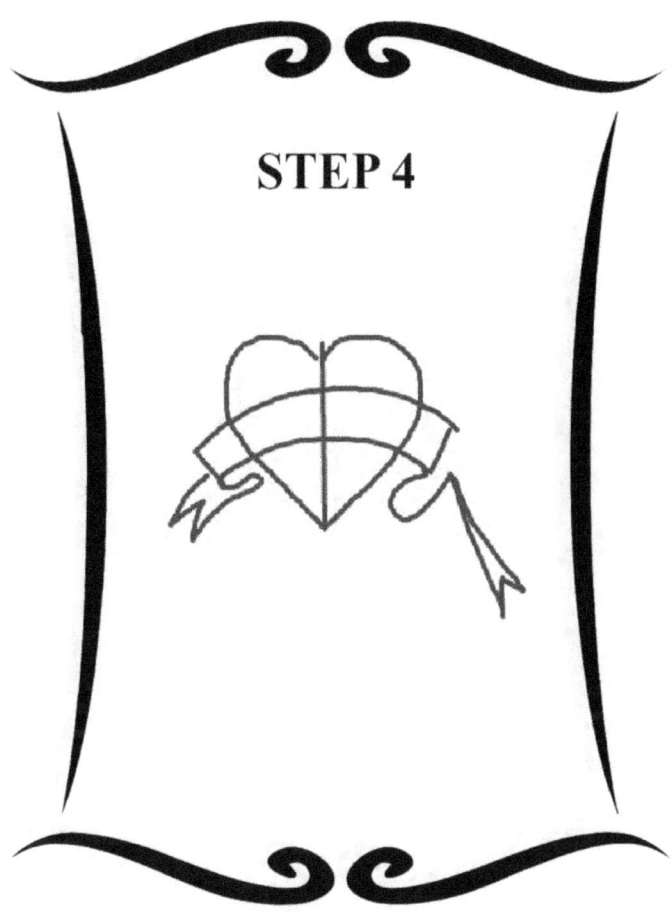

STEP 5

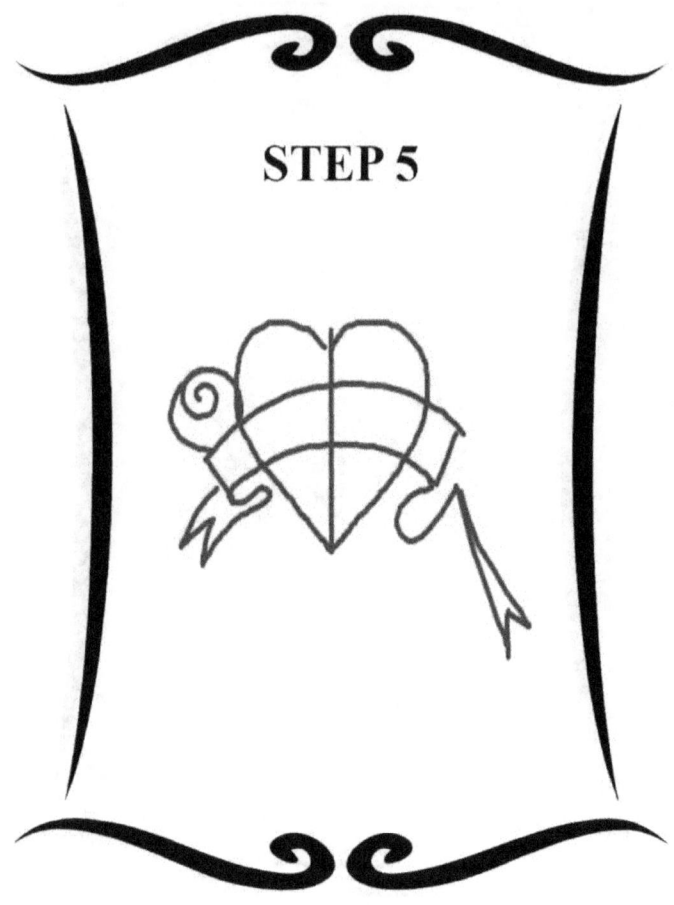

STEP 6

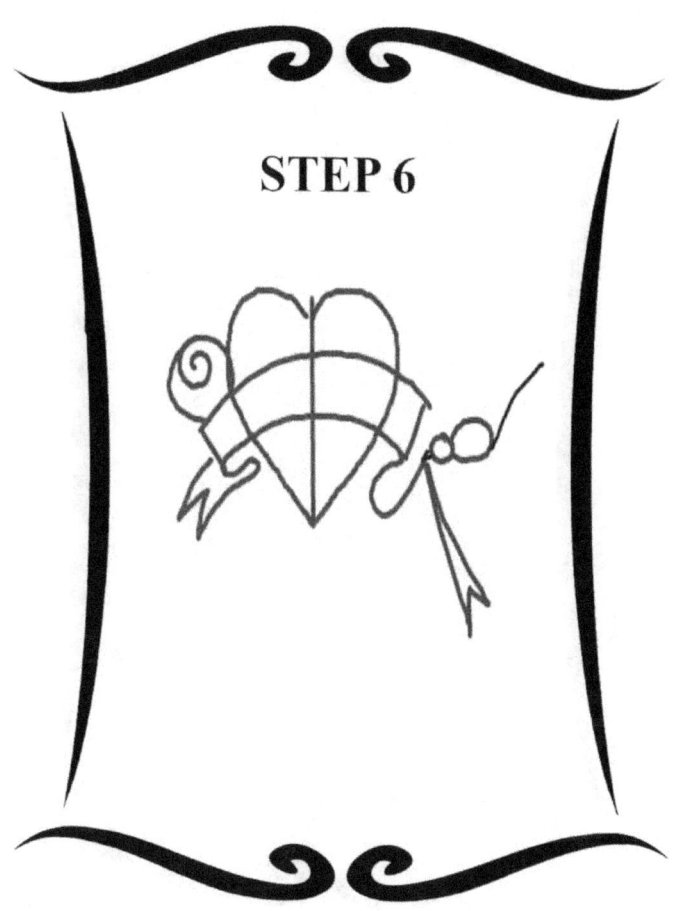

STEP 7

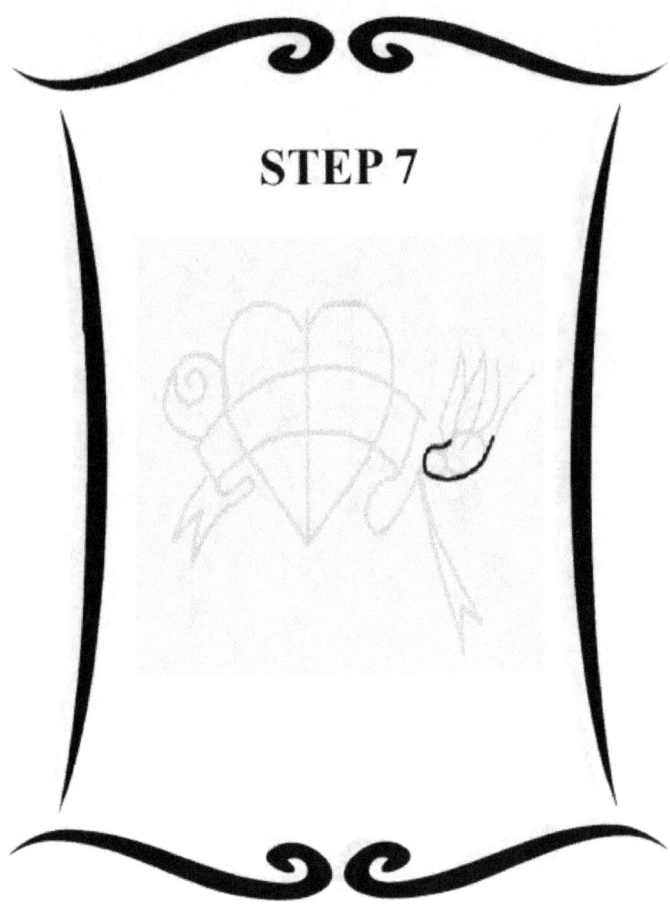

STEP 8

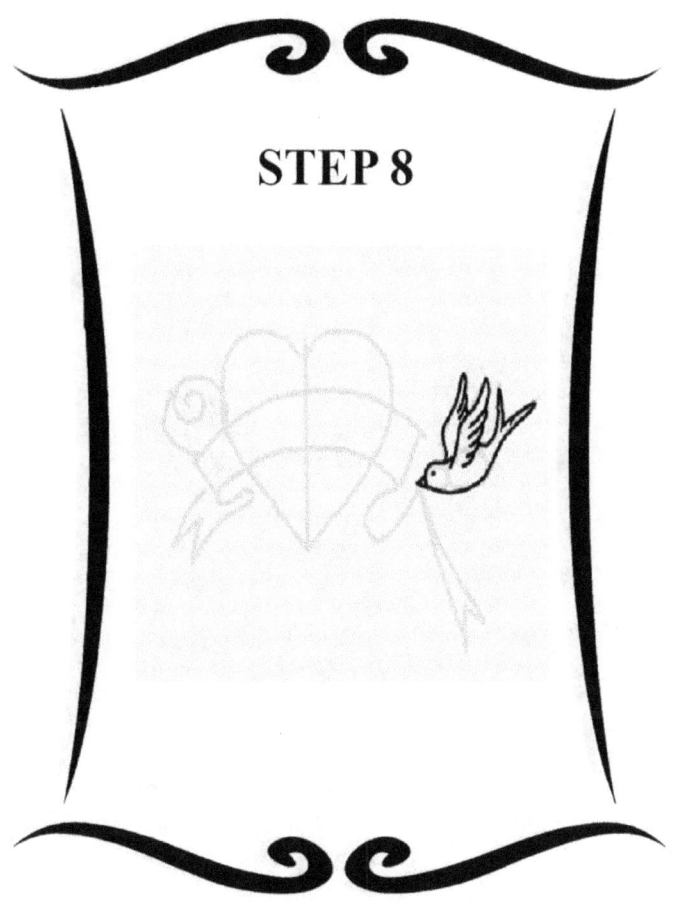

STEP 9

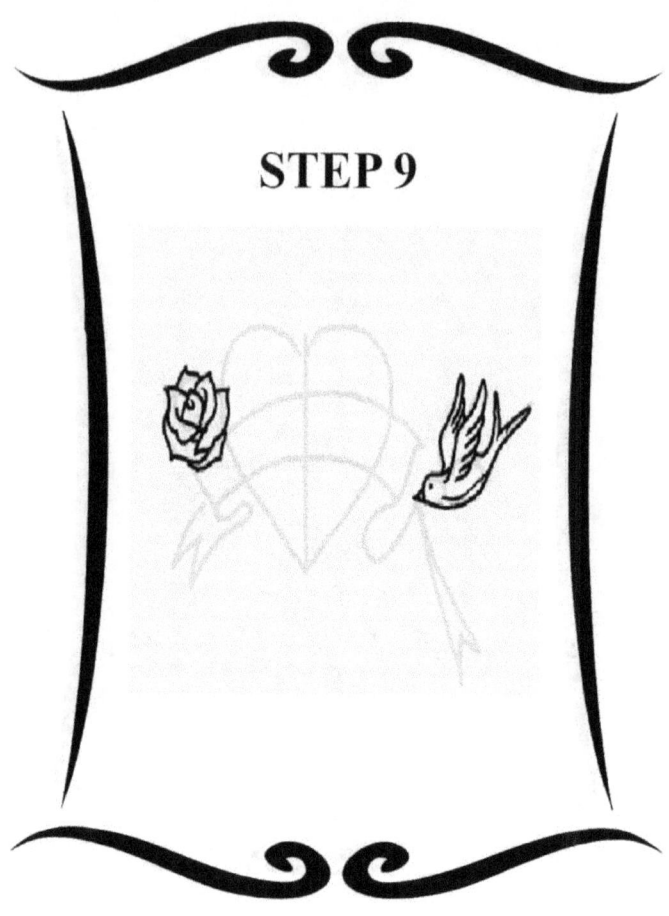

STEP 10

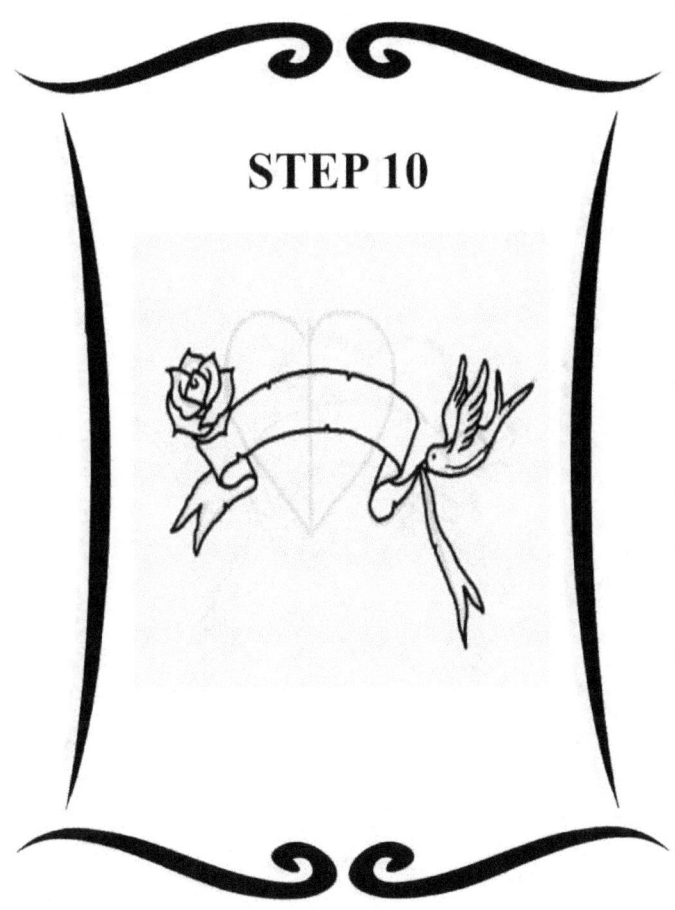

STEP 11

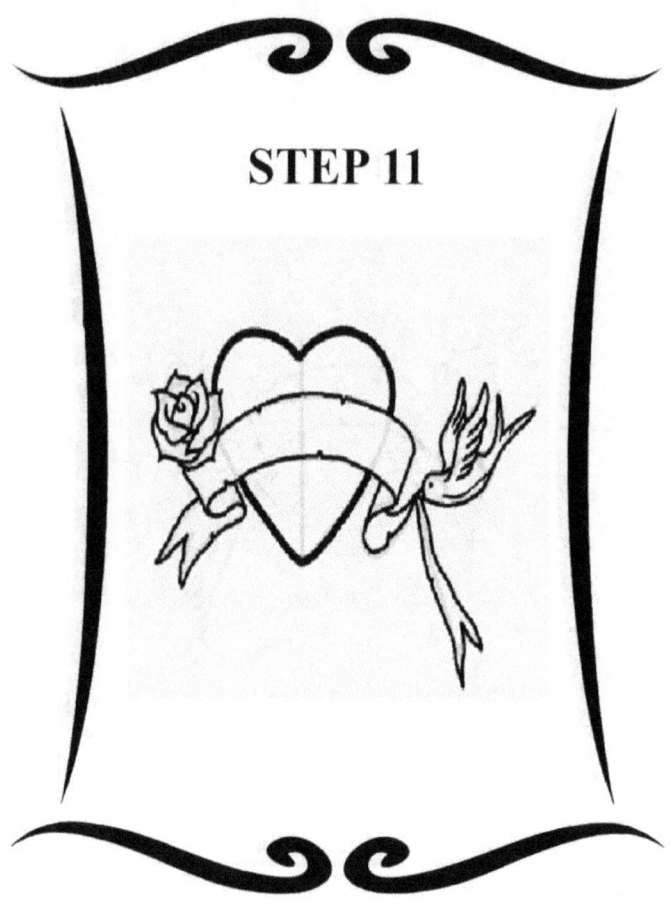

QUILEUTE TATTOO

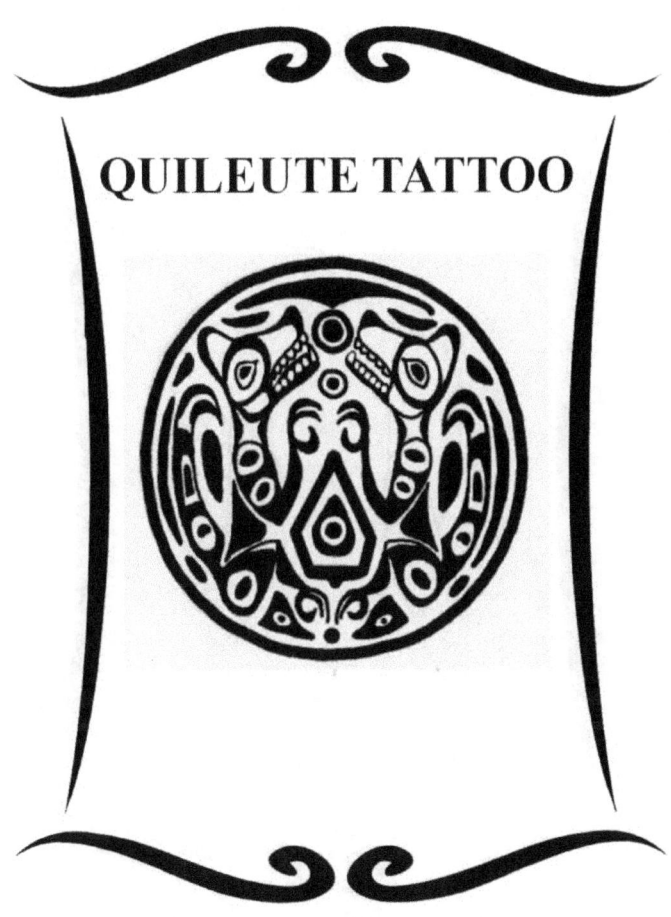

STEP 1

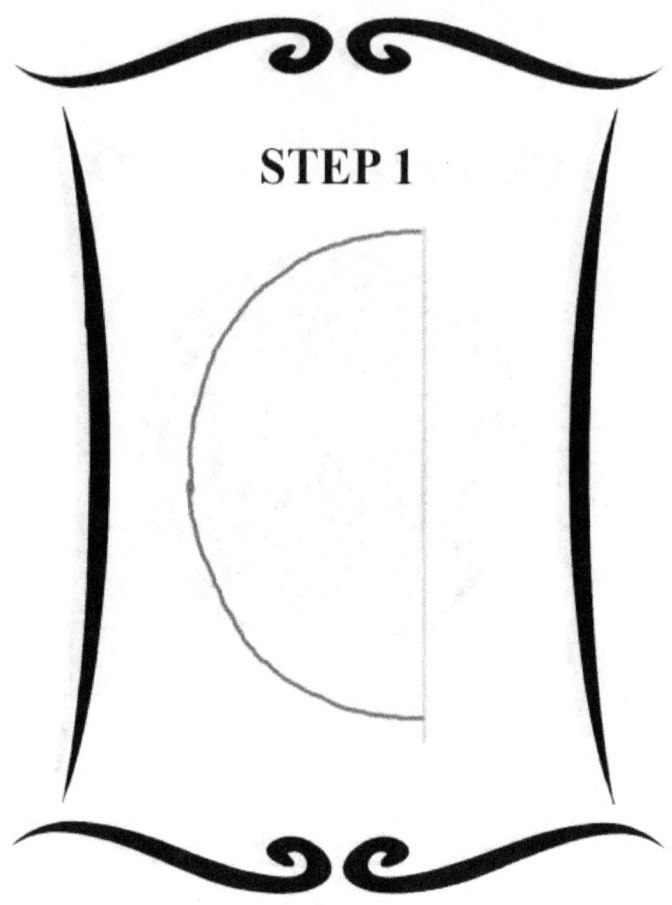

STEP 2

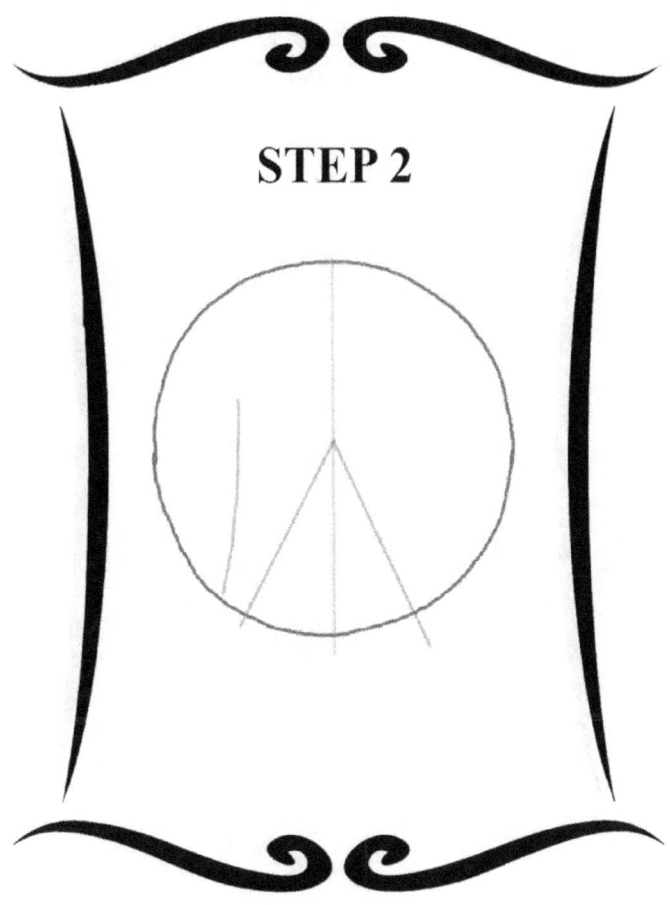

STEP 3

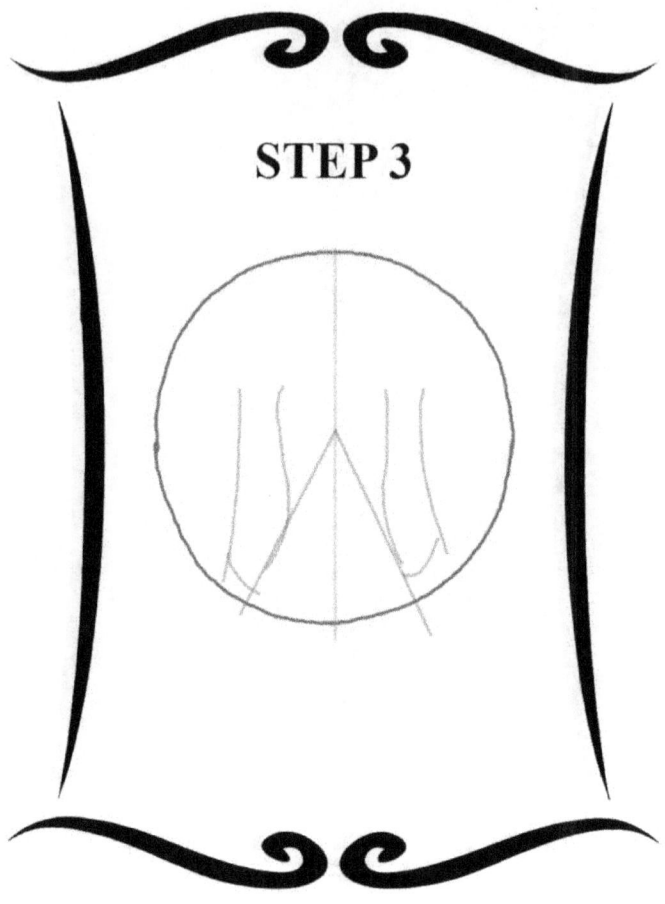

STEP 4

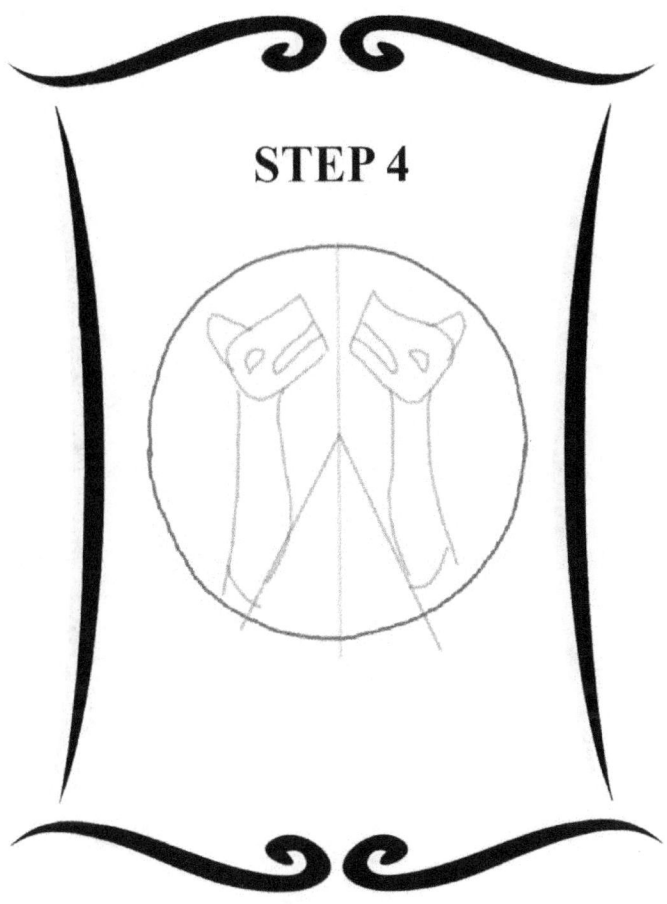

STEP 5

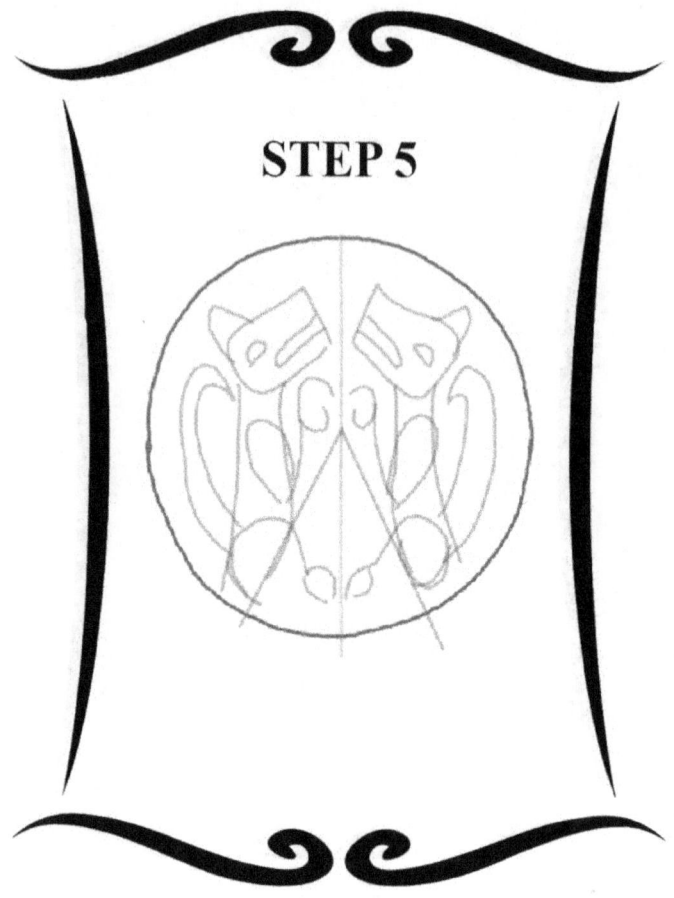

STEP 6

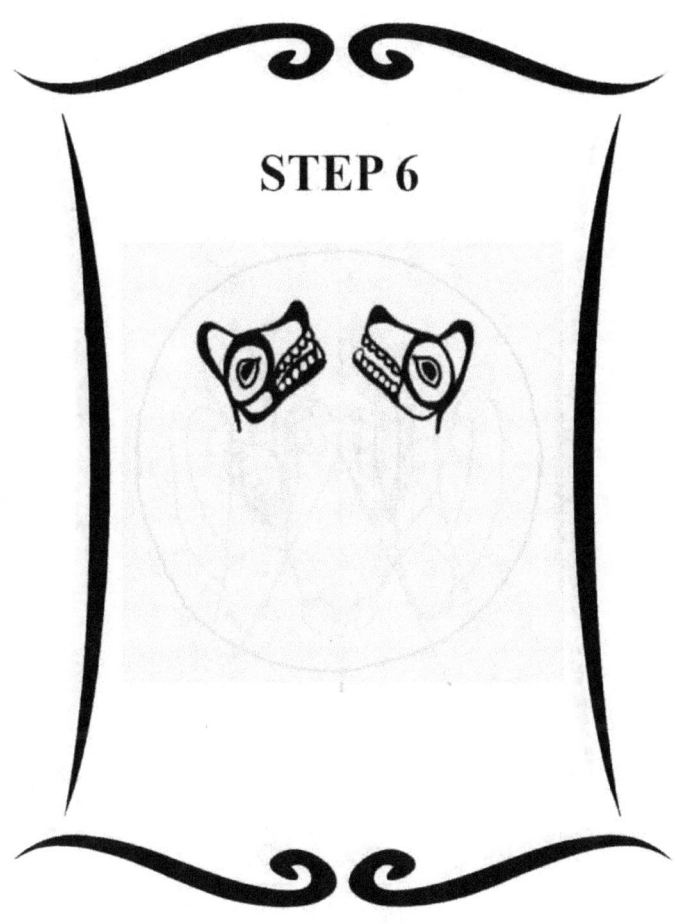

48

STEP 7

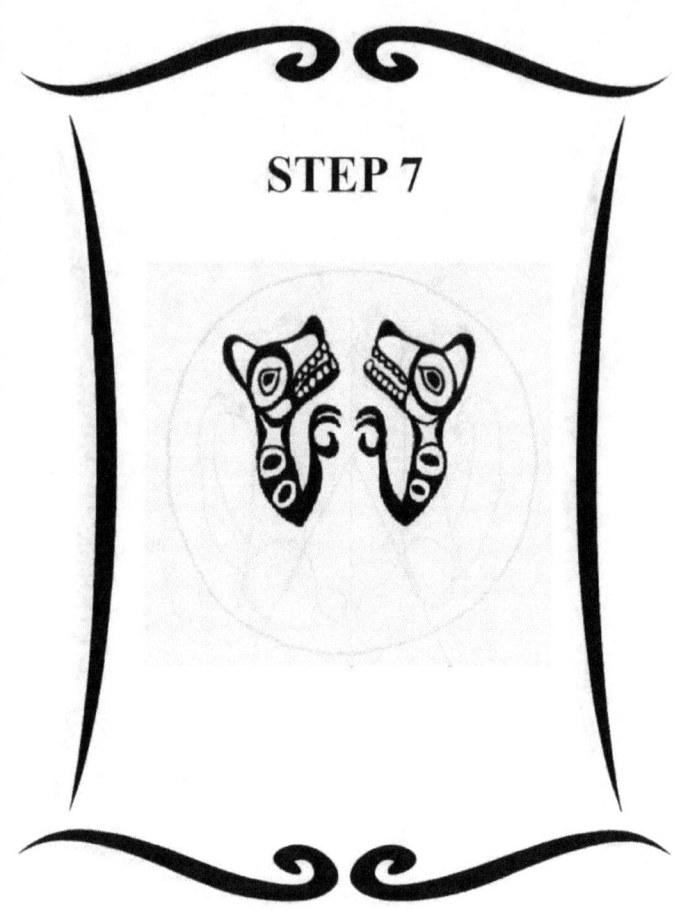

STEP 8

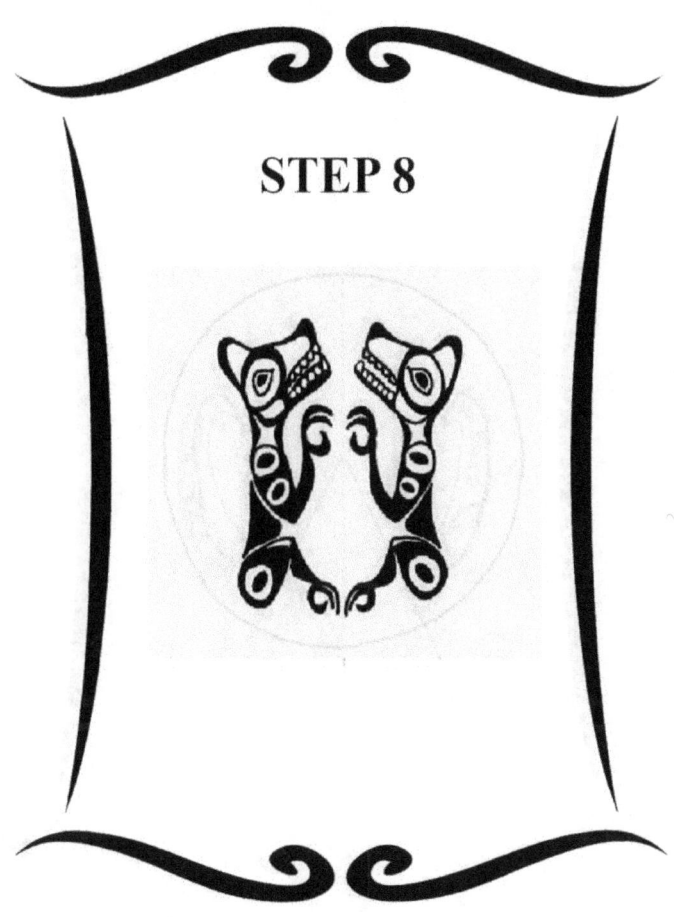

STEP 9

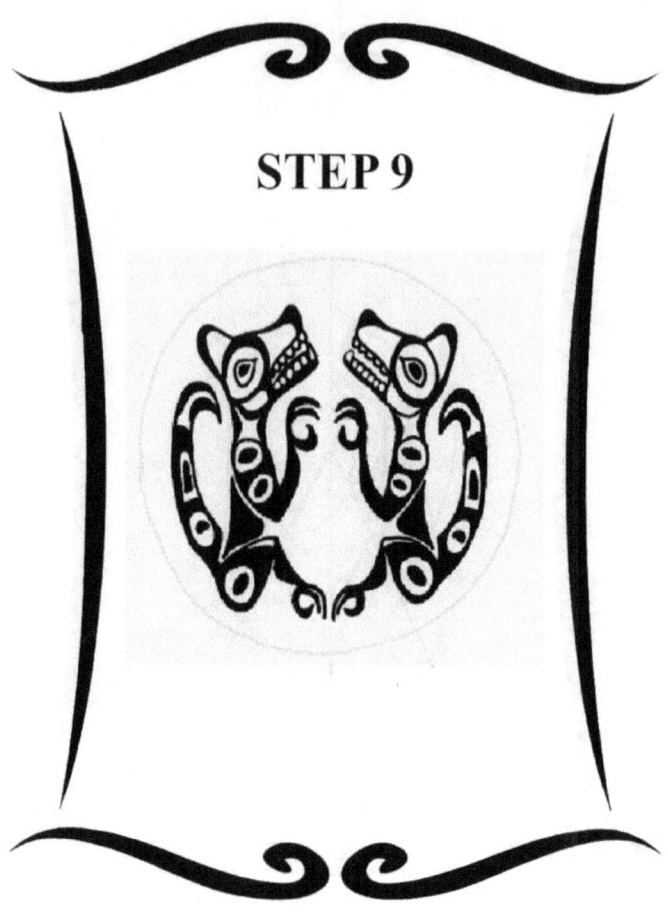

STEP 10

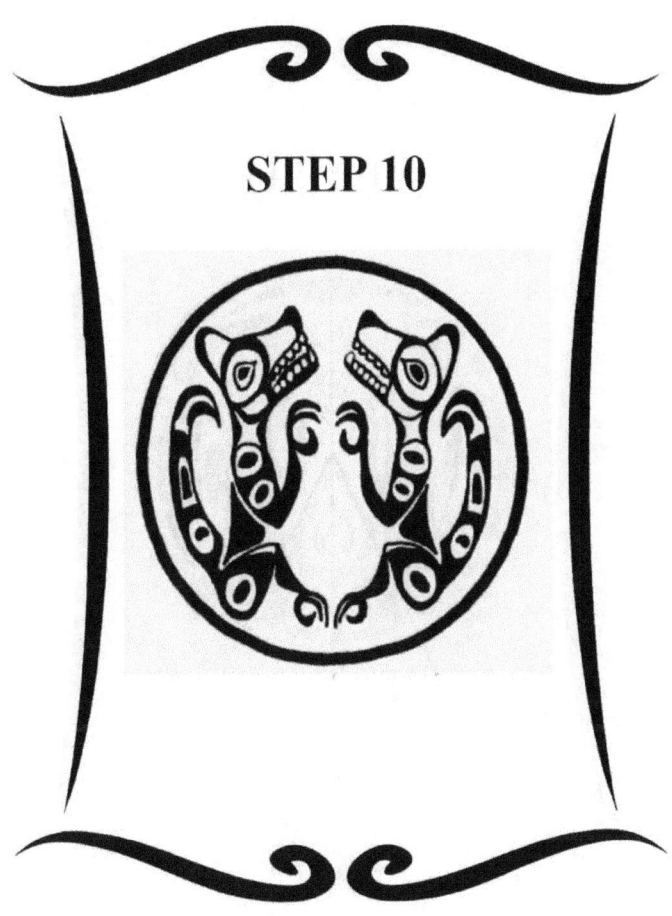

STEP 11

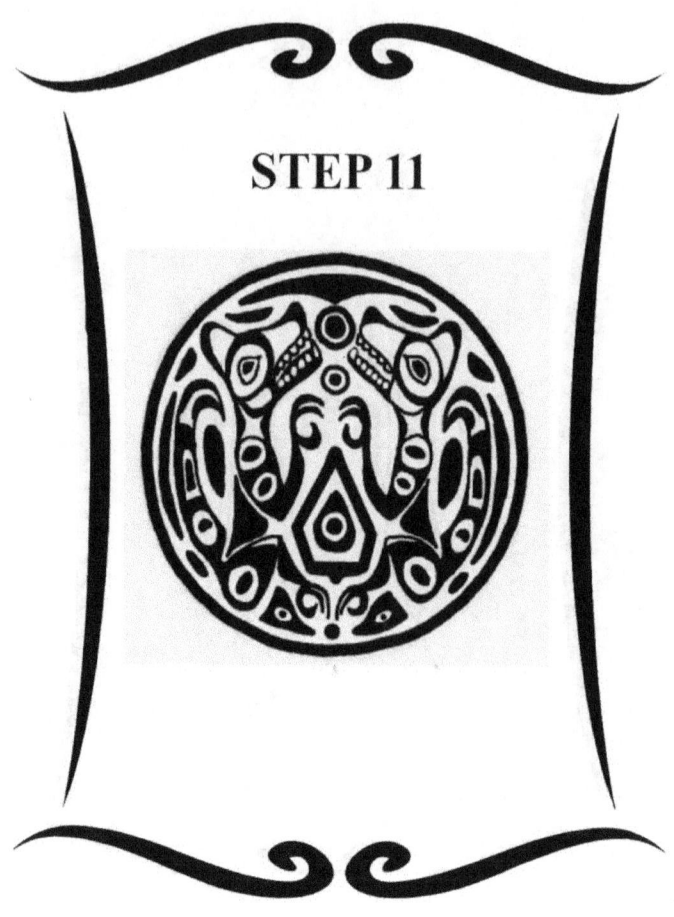

ROSE TATTOO

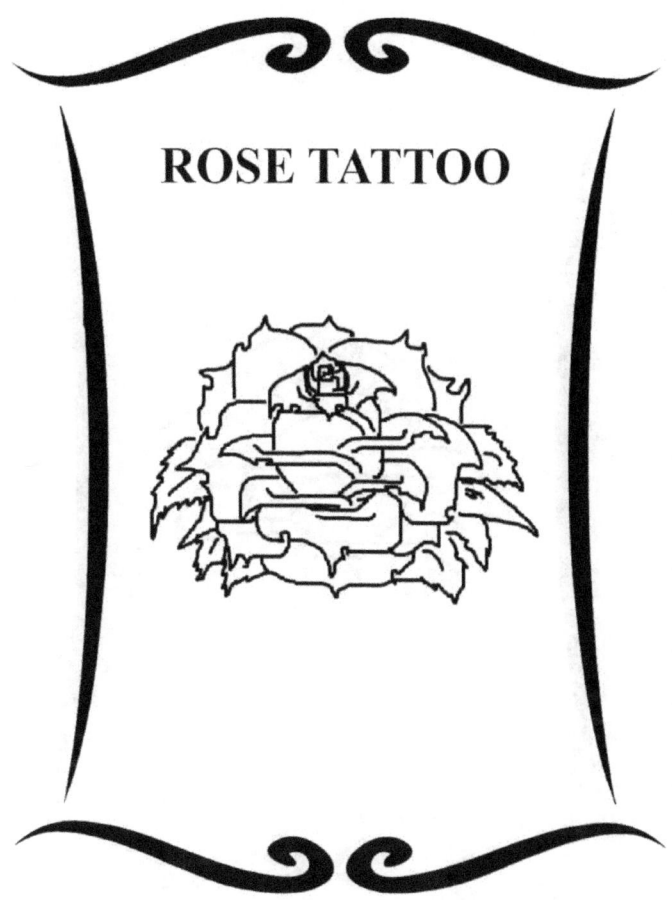

STEP 1

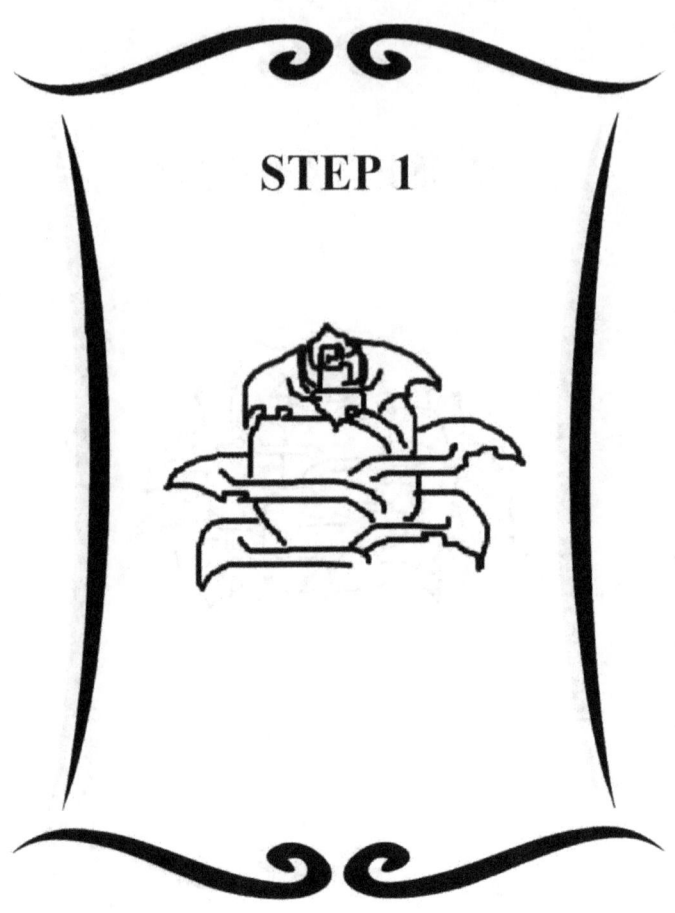

STEP 2

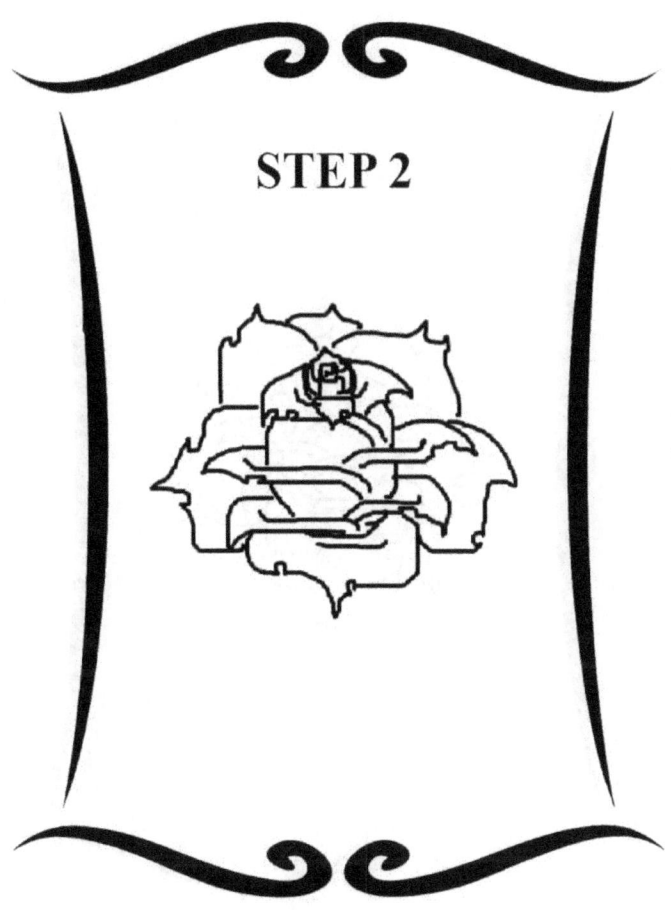

STEP 3

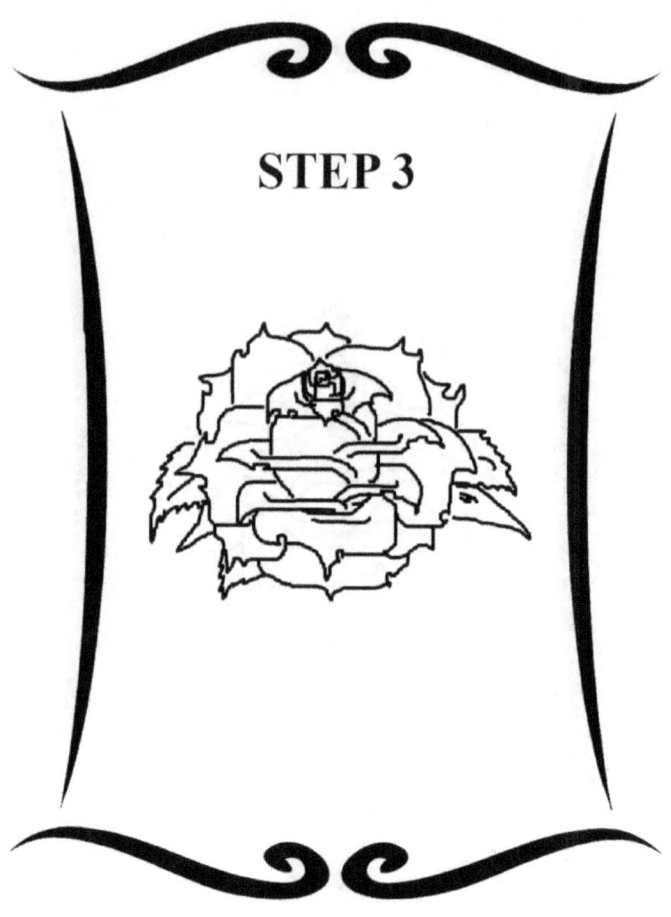

STEP 4

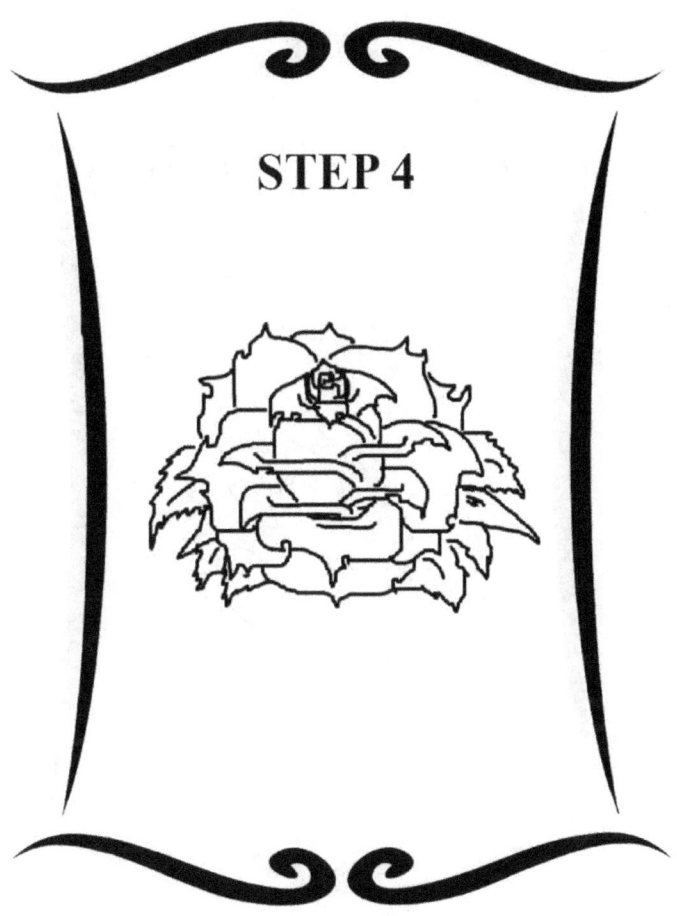

TRIBAL EYE TATTOO

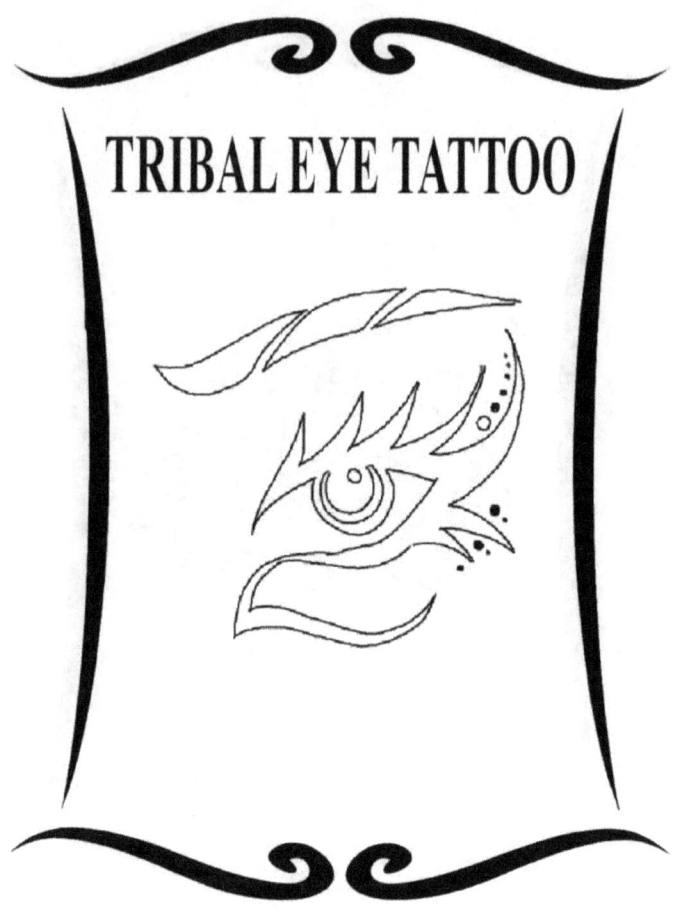

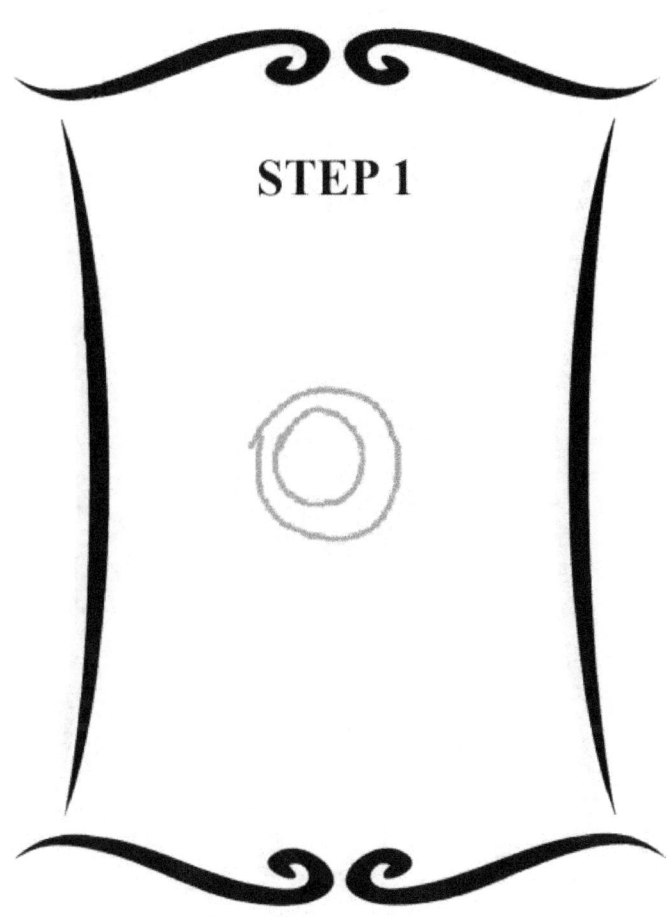

STEP 1

STEP 2

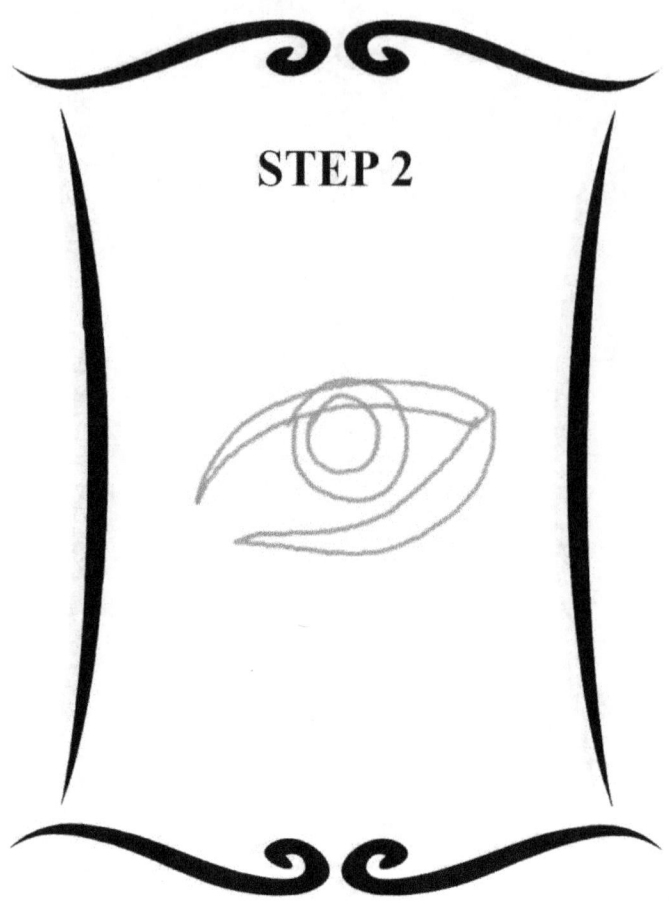

STEP 3

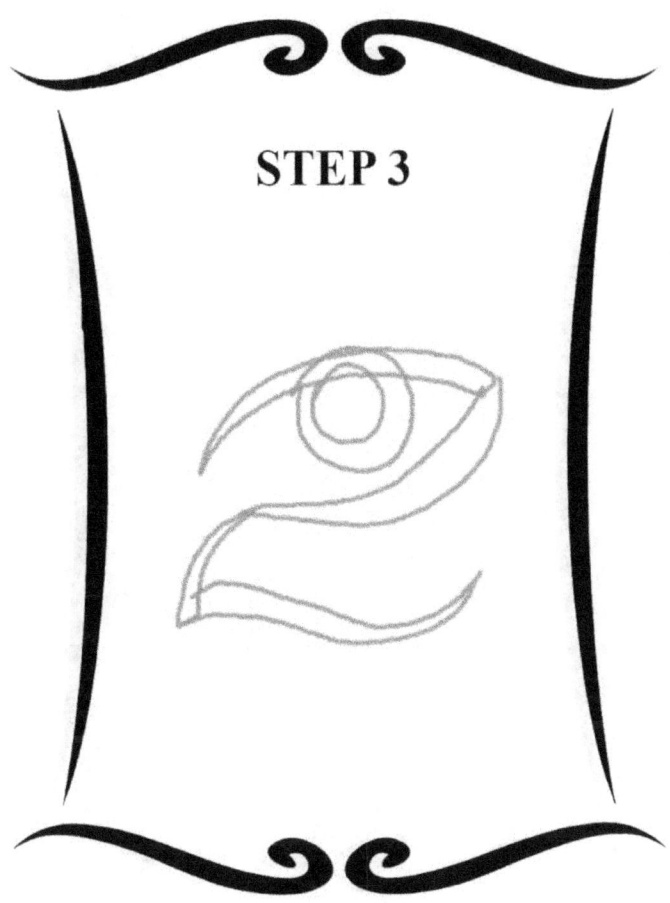

STEP 4

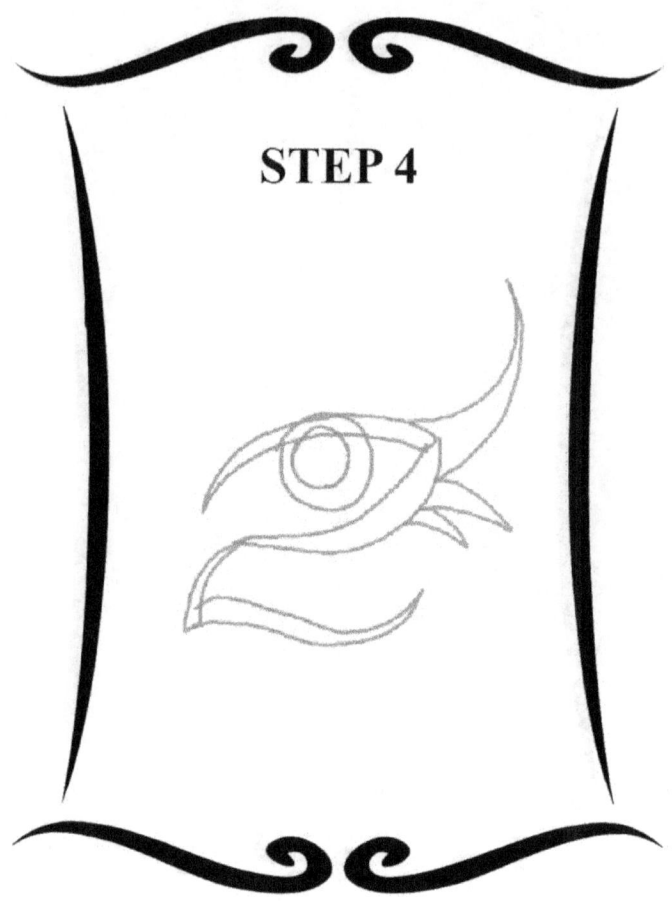

STEP 5

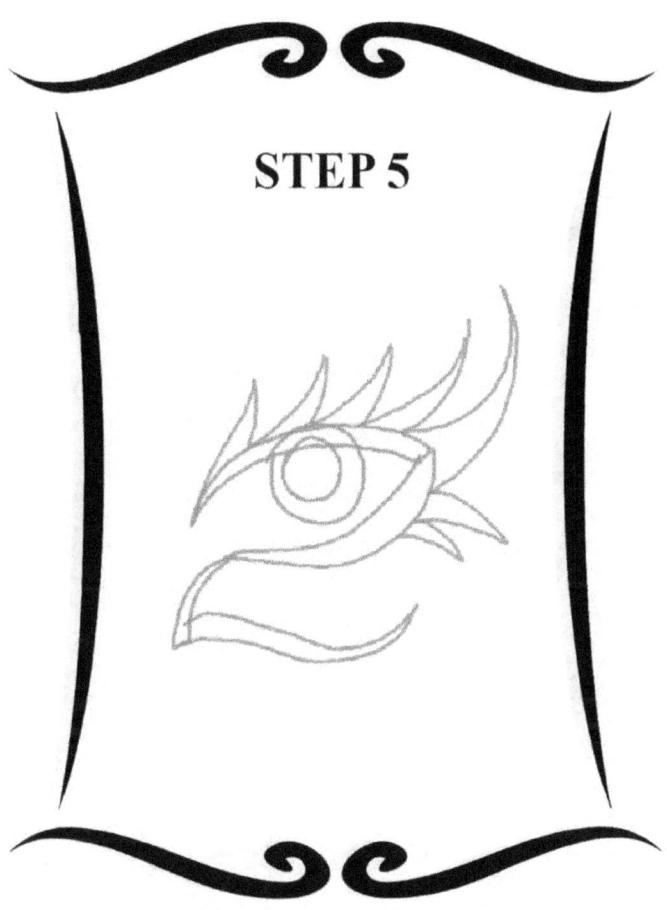

STEP 6

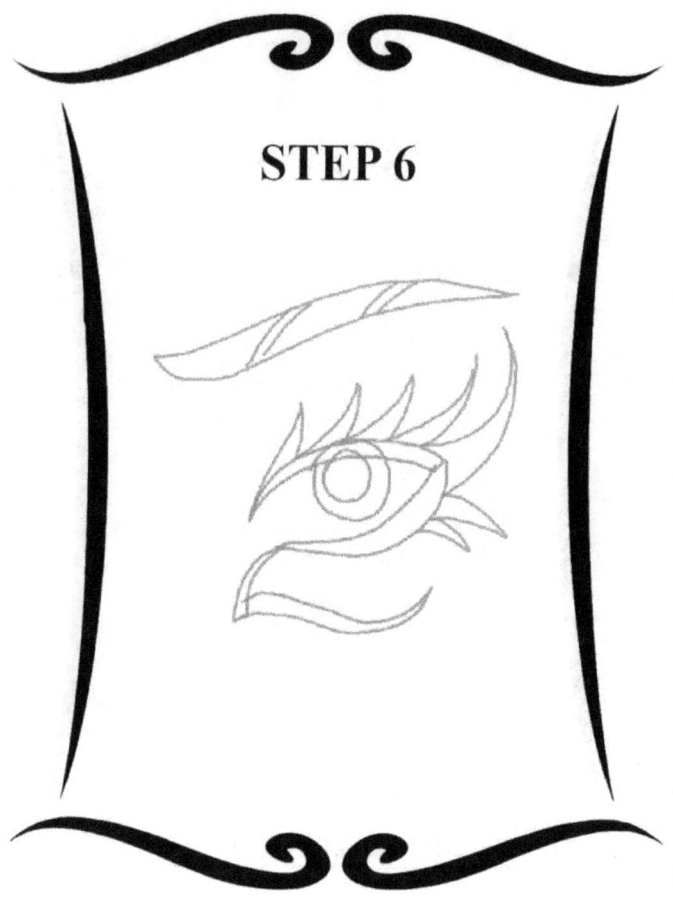

STEP 7

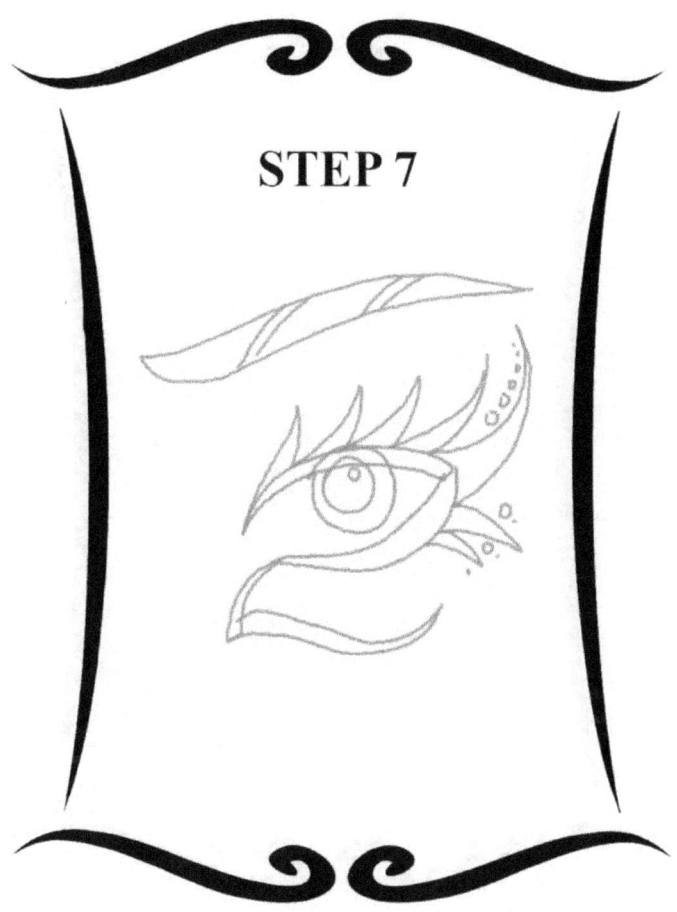

STEP 8

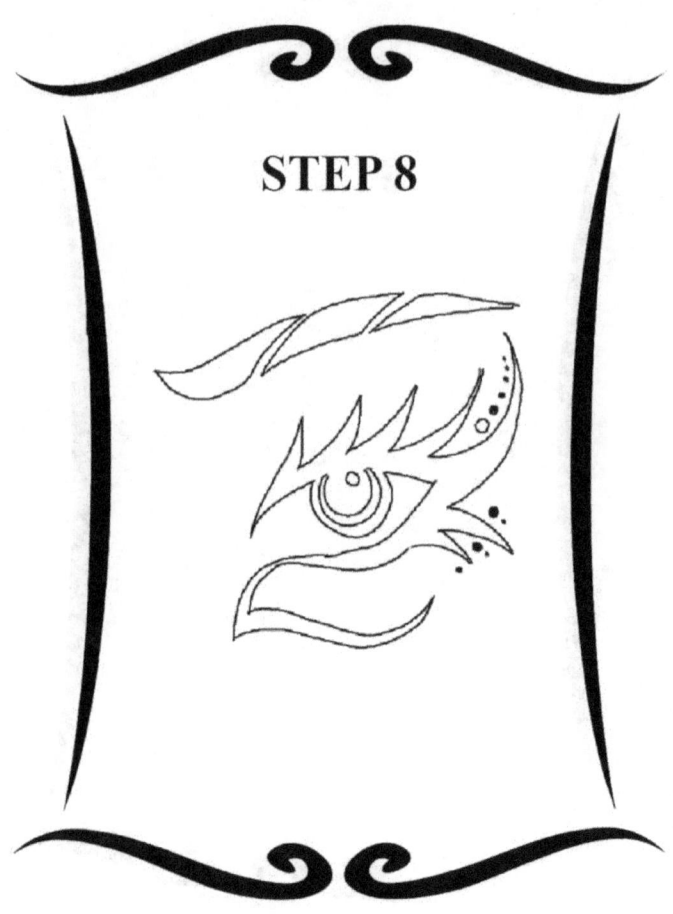

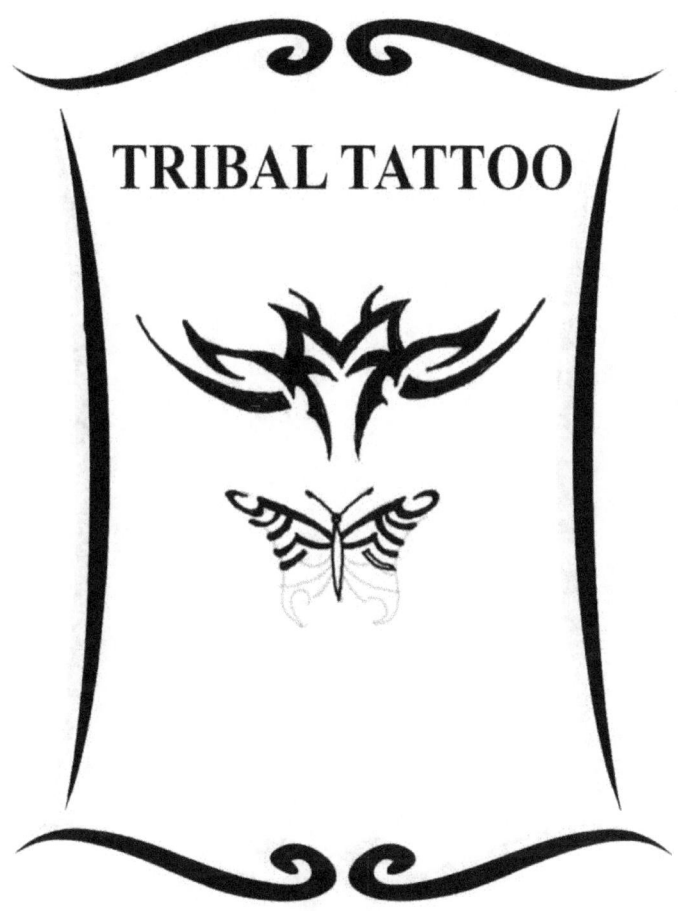

TRIBAL TATTOO

STEP 1

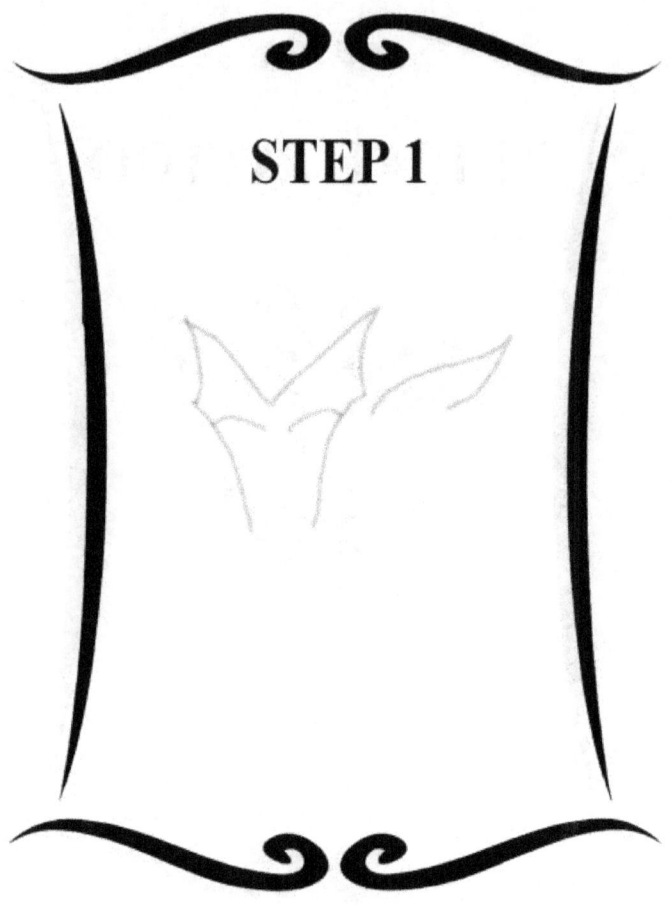

STEP 2

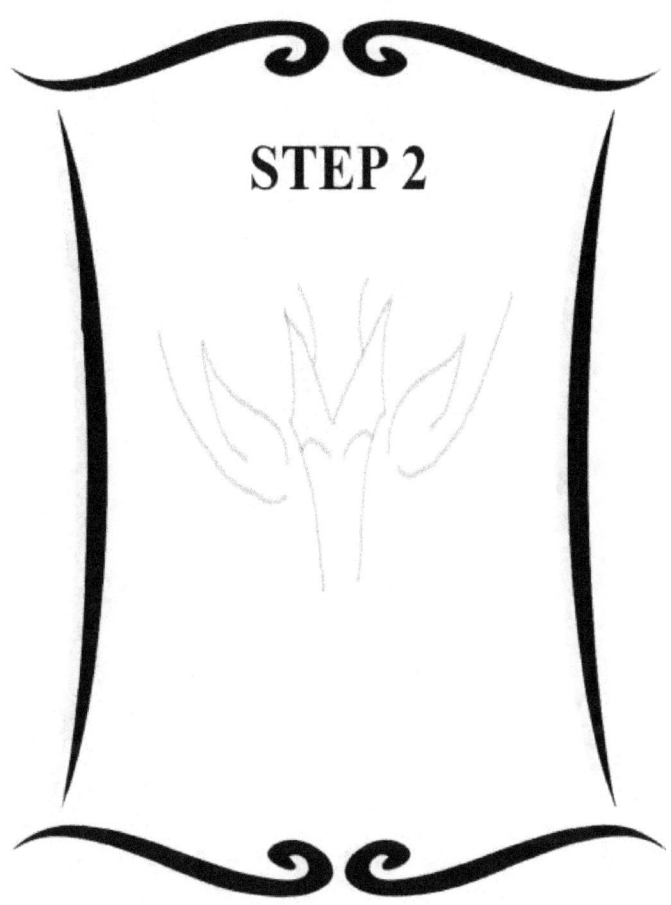

STEP 3

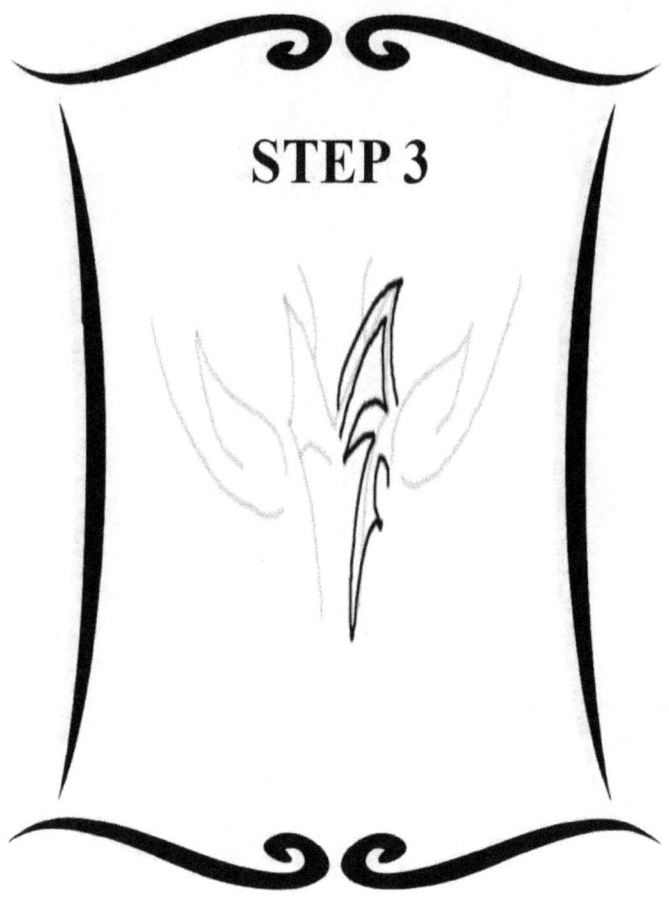

STEP 4

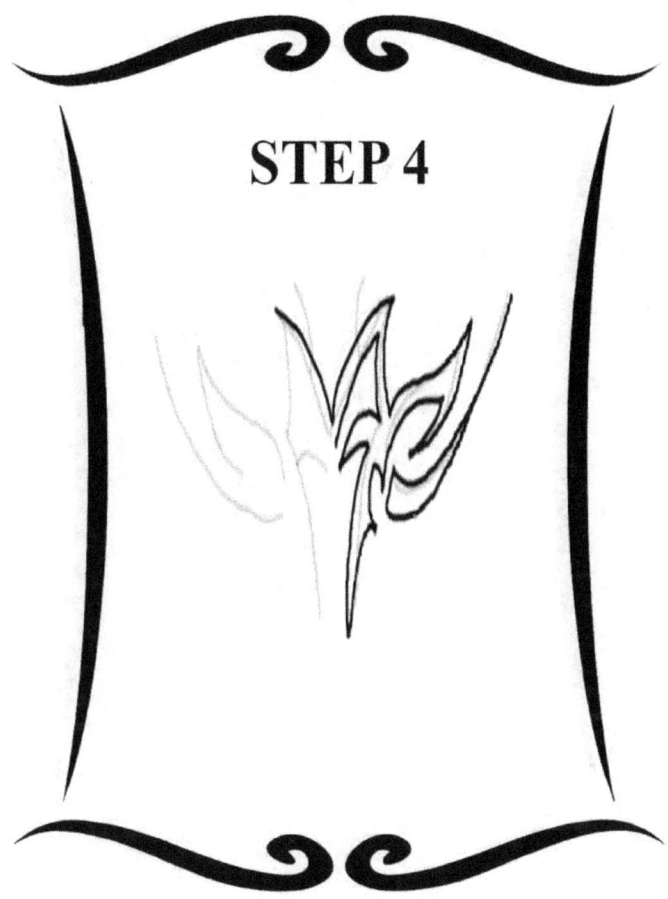

STEP 5

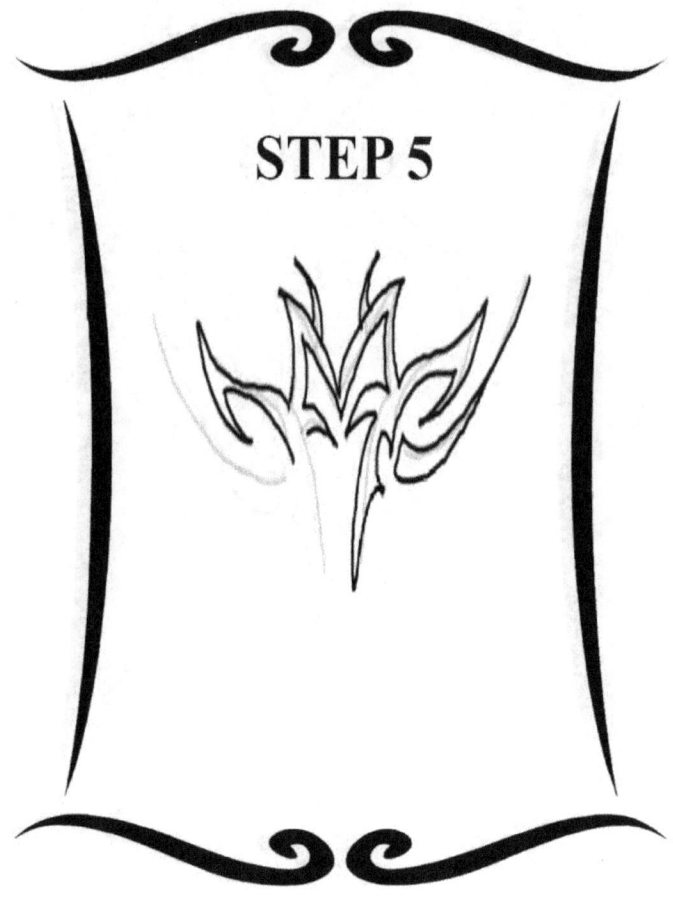

STEP 6

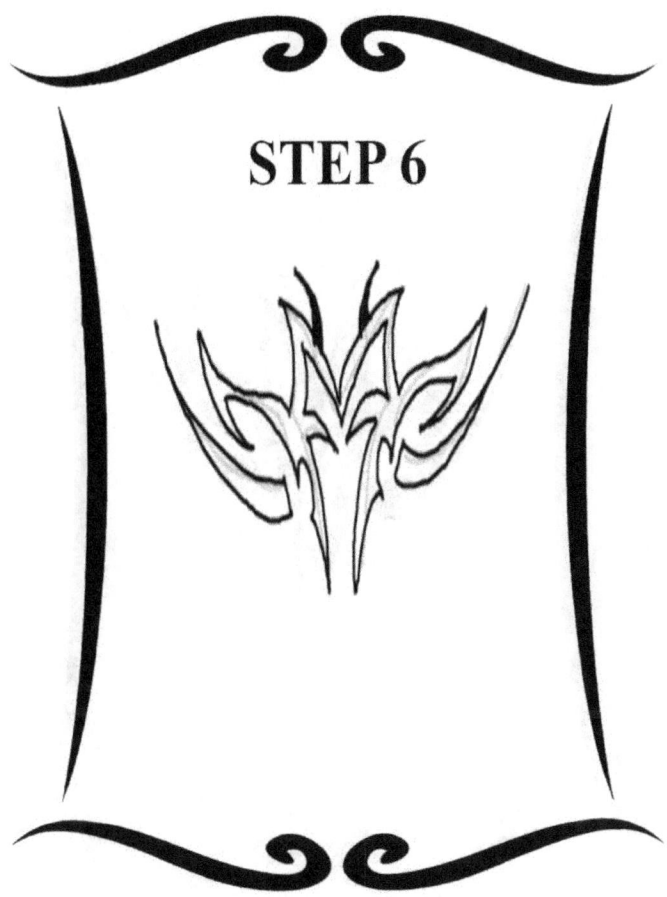

STEP 7

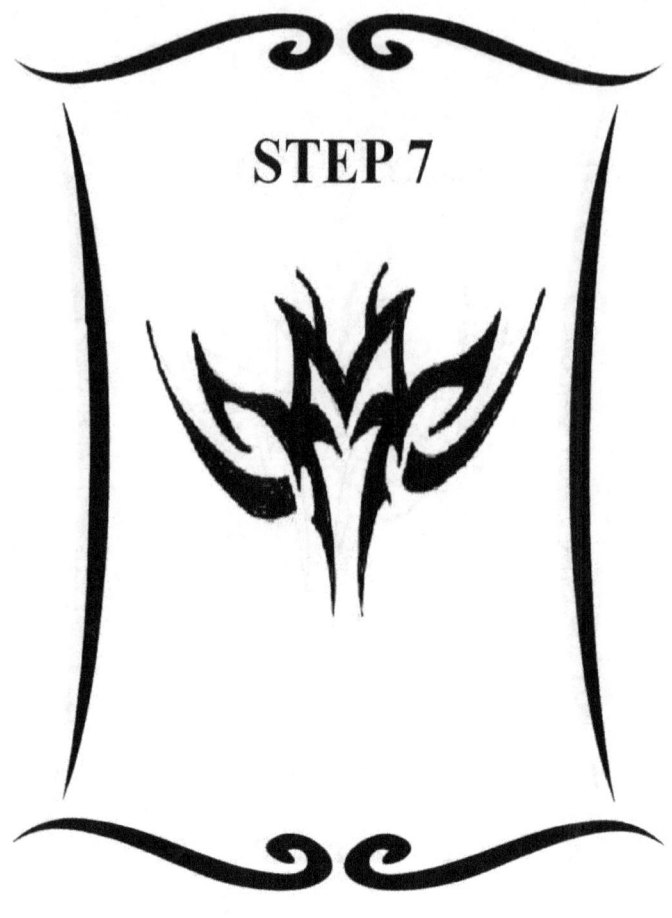

STEP 8

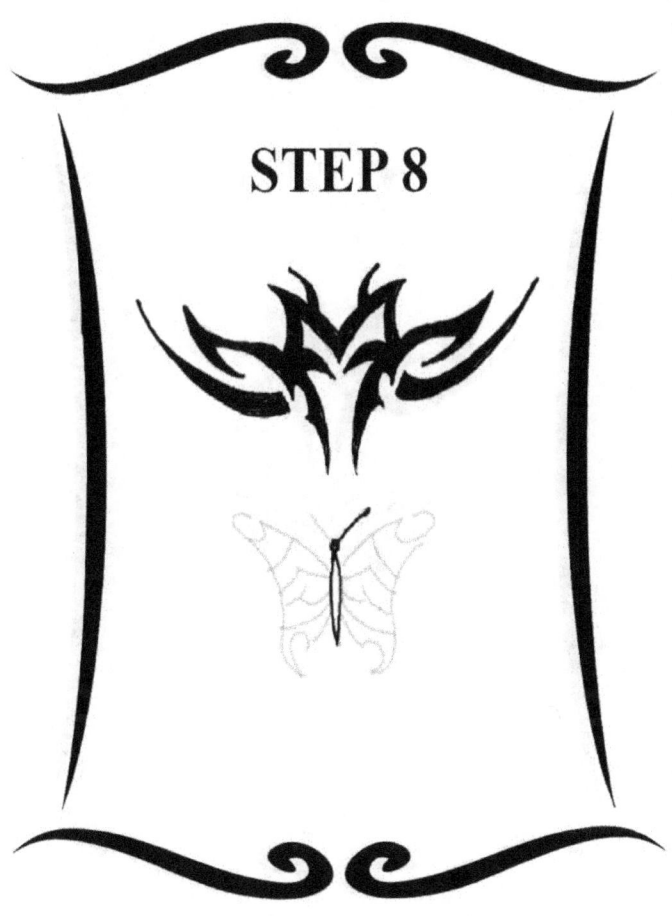

STEP 9

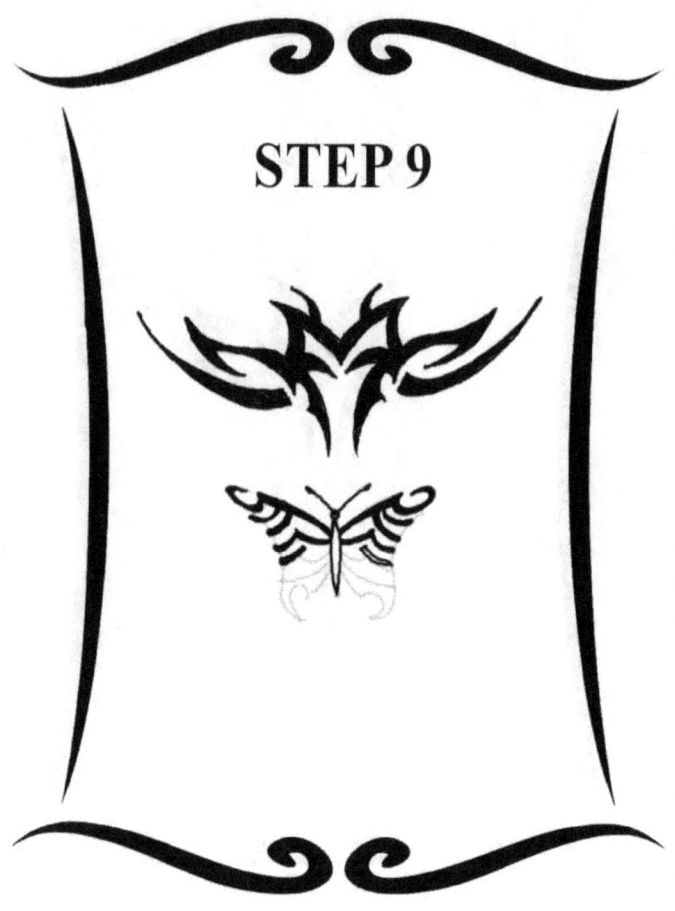